Southern Reformed Theology

Reformed Theology in America
Edited by David F. Wells

---

1. The Princeton Theology
2. Dutch Reformed Theology
3. Southern Reformed Theology

Southern Reformed Theology

Edited by

David F. Wells

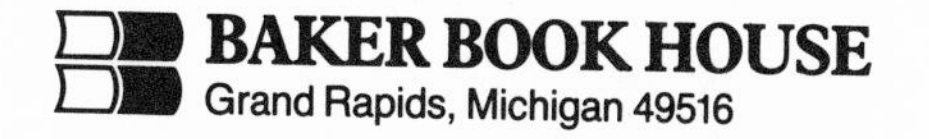
BAKER BOOK HOUSE
Grand Rapids, Michigan 49516

The material in this volume originally comprised part of a book titled *Reformed Theology in America: A History of Its Modern Development*, copyright 1985 by Wm. B. Eerdmans Publishing Company.

Printed in the United States of America

Library of Congress Cataloging-in-Publication Data

Southern Reformed theology / edited by David F. Wells.
p. cm.
"The material in this volume originally comprised part of a book titled Reformed theology in America: a history of its modern development, copyright 1985 by Wm. B. Eerdmans Publishing Company"—T.p. verso.
Other portions of this original work republished under Dutch Reformed theology and Princeton theology.
Bibliography: p.
Includes index.
Contents: The Southern tradition / Morton Smith—Robert Lewis Dabney / Douglas Floyd Kelly—James Henley Thornwell / Luder G. Whitlock, Jr.
ISBN 0-8010-9703-7
1. Reformed Church—Southern States—Doctrines—History. 2. Presbyterian Church—Southern States—Doctrines—History. 3. Calvinism—Southern States—History. 4. Theology, Doctrinal—Southern States—History. 5. Theologians—Southern States—History. I. Wells, David F. II. Smith, Morton H. (Morton Howison), 1923– . III. Kelly, Douglas 1943– . IV. Whitlock, Luder G. V. Reformed theology in America.
BX9424.5.S646S68 1989
230′.5775—dc20 89-6932
CIP

To Roger Nicole
A man of God

CONTENTS

Contributors ix
Preface xi
Introduction: Reformed and American 1
George M. Marsden

1 The Southern Tradition 13
Morton Smith

2 Robert Lewis Dabney 35
Douglas Floyd Kelly

3 James Henley Thornwell 61
Luder G. Whitlock, Jr.

Bibliography 75
Index 91

CONTRIBUTORS

Douglas Floyd Kelly, former editor of the *Journal of Christian Reconstruction,* ministered at the First Presbyterian Church, Dillon, SC, and the First Presbyterian Church, Raeford, NC. Currently he is associate professor of systematic theology, Reformed Theological Seminary, and cotranslator and coeditor of *The Westminster Confession of Faith: A New Edition* (Greenwood, SC: Attic, 1979)

George M. Marsden, professor of the history of Christianity in America at The Divinity School, Duke University, is the author of *Reforming Fundamentalism: Fuller Seminary and the New Evangelicalism* (Grand Rapids: Eerdmans, 1987), *Fundamentalism and American Culture* (New York: Oxford University Press, 1980), and *The Evangelical Mind and the New School Presbyterian Experience* (New Haven: Yale University Press, 1970); coauthor (with Mark Noll and Nathan Hatch) of *The Search for Christian America* (Westchester, IL: Crossway, 1983); and editor of *Evangelicalism and Modern America* (Grand Rapids: Eerdmans, 1984).

Morton Smith has been stated clerk of the General Assembly of the Presbyterian Church in America from 1973 to the present. Formerly professor of systematic theology at Reformed Theological Seminary (Jackson, MS), he is now a faculty member at Greenville (NC) Seminary. He is the author of *Studies in Southern Presbyterian Theology* (Amsterdam: Kampen, 1962) and *How Is the Gold Become Dim* (Jackson, MS: Continuing Presbyterian Church, 1973).

Luder G. Whitlock, Jr., is president of Reformed Theological Seminary (Jackson, MS) and formerly its associate professor of Christian missions.

PREFACE

ONE of the quirks of American theology is that it is frequently unaware of being American. German theology, of course, is the result of the ponderous and enormously thorough German academic machinery from which it has emerged. British theology, with its keen interest in historical accuracy, fair play, and civility, obviously reflects the virtues of the middle and upper-middle classes in which it is largely nurtured. South American theology makes no bones about being South American. It wears its heart on its sleeve. North of the border, however, this is not so. Here, we simply do theology!

If that were really true, then we should expect to find in the various expressions of Reformed theology a striking conformity, for they are all disciplined by the Reformation principles of *sola Scriptura, sola gratia, in solo Christo,* and *sola fide.* What we actually encounter is a most astonishing variety of expression, despite the common ownership of these principles. Immigrants who have come to these shores, nurturing within themselves the Reformed faith on which they were reared, did not melt into the national pot as they were supposed to. Ethnic interests, in fact, were often preserved through language and custom even as a diffuse sense of what it meant to be American also grew in importance. And, along the way, Reformed theologies have struck up alliances with the habits of mind that have prevailed in this or that age as well as being shaped by the towering figures who, from time to time, have arisen above the tradition and given it new cogency, new direction, and sometimes new horizons. American Reformed theology, as a result, is a complex tradition made up of strands and tributaries that are not only diverse but also sometimes quite oblivious to one another.

In 1985 *Reformed Theology in America: A History of Its Modern Development* appeared. To those with eyes to see, it was a thinly disguised *Festschrift* for Roger Nicole, who was celebrating his seventieth birthday that year. But it was also a serious accounting of the Reformed tradition in all of its diversity. I chose what I saw to be the five major streams of Reformed thought: the Princeton theology, the Westminster school, the Dutch schools, the Southern tradition, and neoorthodoxy. Within each of these sections I followed the same pattern of providing readers with a general essay on the school and essays on its two most prominent theologians.

The success that attended the publication of this study was nowhere better attested than in the dozens of letters I received, as well as in the reviews which were published, that complained about this or that group which had been excluded from consideration! All of a sudden I was beset with the knowledge of numerous groups, streams, traditions, and movements that would have liked to have been recognized and felt a little aggrieved that I had not seen fit to include them! It was then that I knew that I had to seek a new publisher for this work once the Eerdmans edition had run its course.

I am deeply grateful for the willingness of Baker Book House to do this. They decided to divide the original study into three smaller books, representing the sections originally published as the Princeton theology, the Dutch schools, and the Southern tradition. (Two essays from the Westminster section—J. Gresham Machen and Cornelius Van Til—have been included with Princeton theology and Dutch schools respectively.) To each volume is appended George Marsden's introduction, and to each is added a bibliography, which was not in the original edition. I wish to thank James Bratt (the Dutch schools), William Yount (the Southern tradition), and Mark Noll (the Princeton theology) for their excellent work.

These three studies will be of particular interest to those who identify themselves with these traditions. I hope, however, that in addition to this anticipated readership there will be many others who look with fresh interest on these works. Those who care about the church, who treat their faith with seriousness, and who long that God's greatness, his sufficiency, and his glory would be more widely owned and celebrated, can only watch the current developments in the evangelical world with growing disquiet. Evangelical faith is showing too many signs of having become secularized, of fragmenting, of regressing to a stage of immaturity that surely raises the question as to how long it can survive as recognizably evangelical in the midst of the furnace of modernity. In the Reformation traditions there is a strength, a virility, a power of correction that needs to be heard again in today's evangelical world, and it is my prayer that in some small way these volumes may contribute to that end.

D.F.W.
Easter, 1989

INTRODUCTION: REFORMED AND AMERICAN

GEORGE M. MARSDEN

WHAT sense does it make in late twentieth-century America to talk about being "Reformed"? For most Americans the word conveys no clear meaning. Very few would think of it as a religious designation at all, and most of those would think it referred to Judaism. Even if, as in the present work, we limit the audience to those who have some notion of "Reformed theology," we are left with the problem that even among such a select group, "Reformed" has numerous differing connotations. In the United States alone there are about a dozen Reformed denominations and perhaps another half-dozen with a Reformed heritage. Within each of the Reformed denominations varieties of meanings are given to being "Reformed." These may reflect European traditions, such as Scottish or Dutch, or continental neoorthodox, as well as a variety of American developments. Each such type includes differing subtypes. For instance, within the Reformed Church in America alone, ten distinct approaches to the Reformed faith have been identified.[1] Differences across denominational lines may be sharper. A strictly confessional member of the Reformed Presbyterian Church in North America (Covenanters) might be most unhappy with the preaching at Robert Schuller's Crystal Cathedral. A fundamentalist Bible Presbyterian would refuse fellowship with almost any member of the United Church of Christ. And within most of the larger Reformed denominations, conservatives and progressives are locked in intense struggles over the true meaning of the faith.

A major purpose of this essay is to cut through the bewildering confusion of the many meanings of "Reformed" by reducing the categories to the three major Reformed emphases that have flourished in the American cultural setting. Not every Reformed heritage can be subsumed under these categories and the categories are ideal types or models rather than fully nuanced representations of the growth of each type. Nonetheless, these are the major subgroups that have been prominent among the Reformed throughout American history. So if we understand something of these three developments and emphases we can gain a fairly good picture of the main varieties of being "Reformed" in the American cultural setting.

Perhaps an illustration from my own experience can make clear the characters of the differences among these major American Reformed traditions. Most of my life I have lived in one or the other of two communities that placed great merit on being Reformed. The central meaning of "Reformed," however, has differed greatly in these two communions. The Orthodox Presbyterians, among whom I was reared, meant by "Reformed" strict adherence to Christian doctrine as contained in the infallible Scriptures and defined by the standards of the Westminster Assembly. Only Christians whose creeds were fully compatible with Westminster's and who viewed subscription to them as paramount were fully within the pale. Other factors were important to Christian life, especially a proper emphasis on the law of God as the central organizing principle in the Westminster formulations. But the operative test for "Reformed" was, with this important practical proviso, always doctrinal.

In the other community in which I have spent many years, the progressive wing of the conservative Christian Reformed Church, being "Reformed" is also taken seriously, but with very different meaning. There, a "Reformed" Christian is one who has a certain view of the relationship of Christianity to culture. She or he must affirm the lordship of Christ over all reality, see Christian principles as applicable to all areas of life, and view every calling as sacred. Although subscription to the authority of the Bible and classic Reformed creeds is significant in this community, the stronger operative test for admission is support for separate Christian schools at all levels (except, oddly, the graduate university), where the "Reformed" world-and-life view can be exemplified and taught.

I have also spent some time at institutions of mainstream American evangelicalism, such as Trinity Evangelical Divinity School and Fuller Theological Seminary, where one finds still another meaning to being "Reformed." In this context being "Reformed" must be understood in the framework of being "evangelical." "Evangelical" is a word with a more elusive meaning than "Reformed." Basically it refers to anyone who promotes proclamation of the gospel of salvation through the atoning work of Christ and has a traditional high view of Scripture alone as authority. Evangelicalism is thus much larger than just the Reformed tradition. Within American evangelicalism, however, there is an important subgroup that might be called "card-carrying" evangelicals.[2] These are persons who think of themselves primarily as "evangelicals" and who, as such, identify at least as much with evangelicalism as a movement as with their own formal denomination. Billy Graham, *Christianity*

Today, Eternity, Inter-Varsity Christian Fellowship, Wheaton College and its imitators, and seminaries such as Trinity, Fuller, and Gordon-Conwell have been prototypes of this influential interdenominational evangelicalism.

In this evangelical fellowship the dominant theological tradition is Reformed. It is by no means, however, the only tradition. One trait of this type of being "Reformed," unlike the other two, is that it is tolerant of diversity to the point of keeping close fellowship with persons of other traditions. The operative tests for fellowship among the Reformed in such communities are those of the broader American evangelical-pietist tradition—a certain style of emphasis on evangelism, personal devotions, Methodist mores, and openness in expressing one's evangelical commitment. To be "Reformed" in this setting means to find in Reformed theology the most biblical and healthiest expression of evangelical piety.

The differing emphases of these three communities suggest that in America there are at least three major meanings to being "Reformed." There are, of course, also a number of other Reformed traditions and styles in America. These include the southern, ethnically and racially defined groups, smaller denominations, progressive Reformed in mainline denominations, and some neoorthodox. Nonetheless, the three we have begun with suggest classically distinct types of emphasis that give us some working categories. Many of the developments of America's Reformed groups can be understood as variations on these typical themes.

For convenience' sake, we shall designate these three types as doctrinalist, culturalist, and pietist.[3] In doing so, it is important to remark again that the terminology refers to "ideal types" or descriptive models emphasizing one dominant trait. In reality all three groups typically embody the traits dominant among the other two. Thus a "pietist" is not typically a person who is lax in doctrine or lacking in cultural concern. Similarly, to call people doctrinalists or culturalists does not imply lack of the other two traits.

The Puritan Stock

The oldest major Reformed community in America was the Puritan, which combined strong elements of each of these emphases. Stress on strict Calvinism helped distinguish these early American settlers from their Arminian Anglican opponents. And Reformed orthodoxy was retained in most New England pulpits for at least a century and a half, to the time of the Revolution.[4] Puritans were also characterized by intense piety, often keeping close records of their spiritual health. Moreover, New England's Puritans were America's most successful Reformed culture builders. Virtually free from outside control during their formative first half-century, they built the closest thing humanly possible to their conception of a biblical kingdom. This impressive effort had a lasting impact on the ideals of American civilization. It is ironic that "Reformed" has so little meaning in America today when in fact the culture has been so shaped by that heritage.

The lasting culture-shaping impact of seventeenth-century Puritanism is rivaled by the long-term influence of its eighteenth-century style of piety, epitomized by the Great Awakening. The eighteenth century was generally an era of widespread resurgent pietism, emphasizing personal commitment to the Savior more than Christian culture building. The Great Awakening in New England was part of a wider Protestant pietist awakening that had begun in Germany and spread to most of the Protestant world. In England its largest manifestation was in Methodism. In America it appeared first primarily as pietist revivalism in Reformed churches.

At the height of the first surge of the Great Awakening in America, around 1740, the classic patterns of American Reformed divisions began to emerge. By this time the other major Reformed group, the Scotch-Irish and Scottish Presbyterian, was on the scene. The often changing relations of the Scottish churches to the state, and the sometimes troubled colonial experiences of the Scotch-Irish in the north of Ireland, fostered among Presbyterians in America varieties of views, or perhaps an ambivalence, concerning culture shaping. They inherited the Calvinist impulse to establish a Christian commonwealth; but they also had enough experience of religious oppression to be suspicious of religious establishments, especially when they were living, as in America, under British rule. The Christian commonwealth would be built by persuasion and education.[5]

The symbol of Presbyterian distinctiveness and unity was thus not a social-political program (except that they were militantly anti-British during the Revolution) but doctrinal orthodoxy. Strict confessionalism was a major trait of the largest party of Scotch-Irish and Scottish Presbyterians from their first appearance in the colonies. Presbyterianism in America, however, was from the outset fed by some other streams, not of Scottish but of English origin. English Presbyterianism itself had become tolerant of doctrinal diversity by the early eighteenth century. More importantly, New England Puritans, especially those in Connecticut, viewed themselves as close allies of Presbyterianism in the Middle Colonies and in the early eighteenth century were providing the newly formed (ca. 1706) Presbyterian Church with personnel and leaders. By the time of the Great Awakening, the New England party was closely linked with the more pietistic revivalist group of the Presbyterians. In

1741 this revivalist "New Side" group split from the antirevivalist Scotch-Irish or Scottish "Old Side."

Remarkably, these two Presbyterian "sides" reunited in 1758, thus suggesting that pietist revivalism and doctrinalist confessionalism were compatible. But the tension between these two emphases repeatedly reemerged. The classic instance was in the Old School/New School schism of 1837-38, in many ways a repetition of the Old Side/New Side conflict. The Old School was clearly the stronghold of Scotch-Irish and Scottish elements and found its unity in strict confessionalism. The New School, on the other hand, represented an alliance of more strongly pietist or prorevivalist Presbyterians with New England Congregationalists.

The Growth of Reformed Branches

By this time, however, a number of other issues surrounded this renewed confrontation between confessionalist and pietist axes. The New School was the more typically American of the two groups, its distinctive characteristics reflecting the tendencies of the ethos of the dominant American evangelicalism. This meant that they were more tolerant of theological innovation and variety than had been their predecessors in the seventeenth- and eighteenth-century American Reformed camps. This doctrinal latitude, however, was not a liberalism that involved intentional concessions to secularism (as in later modernism). Rather, it was an outgrowth of pietist zeal for revivalism. In politically liberal America, such zeal translated into some mildly anti-Calvinist (or semi-Pelagian) doctrines emphasizing an unaided human ability voluntarily to accept the revivalists' gospel message with its culminating summons of "choose ye this day." Such doctrinal innovations were held more closely in check by the New School Presbyterians than by their revivalist Congregationalist allies, such as Charles G. Finney. Moreover, they propounded these innovations in the name of greater faithfulness to Scripture alone, as opposed to what some saw as an unhealthly traditionalism of the Old School.

Openness to practical innovation also characterized the New School pietist strand of the heritage. Finney's "New Measures" for promoting revival in the manner of the high-pressure salesman were only the most prominent examples of evangelicalism's openness to departures from tradition. The spread of gospel music perhaps best exemplified the new evangelical style. Especially notable was a new emphasis on personal experience. Controversial also among the Presbyterians was the New School enthusiasm for working through ecclesiastically independent societies (what are now called parachurch agencies) for missions, evangelism, publication, education, and social reform.

This latter issue of social reform was creating a new source of controversy concerning what it meant to be "Reformed," a debate over what we are calling its culturalist heritage. Prior to the nineteenth century, questions concerning social reform had not been conspicuous, divisive issues. Until that time almost all the Reformed groups seem to have been working on the basis of a vaguely formulated, but deeply entrenched, tradition that, ideally, the religion of a nation should be exclusively Reformed. So they assumed that being Reformed accordingly involved transforming the moral ethos and legal system of a people so that it should comport with God's law. The Puritans, as we have seen, worked these principles out most fully in practice. By the early nineteenth century, however, these Reformed principles had to be translated to fit a pluralistic and democratic situation. The question therefore became that of how much emphasis the Reformed Churches should put on shaping the legal structures of a society they did not otherwise control. Was it not the case that the true mission of the church was to proclaim a pure gospel and be a model moral subcommunity within the larger community, leavening it rather than attempting to legislate morality for all?

Finding answers to these questions was complicated by the fact that sometimes the resolution to moral issues could have as much to do with where one stood politically as it did what theological principles one held. Thus, whereas regarding Sabbath observance most nineteenth-century Reformed groups could unite in supporting legislation, on the issue of slavery they were sharply divided. Moreover, opinions on the slavery issue varied strikingly with geography. In the deep South, Reformed people were adamantly opposed to any interference with the practice of black slavery and emphasized aspects of the tradition that favored confining the activities of the church to strictly "spiritual" issues. In New England, by contrast, Reformed Christians often took the lead in insisting that the churches should unrelentingly urge the state to enact immediate emancipation. In the upper South and the lower North, opinions were more varied and often more nuanced. New School Presbyterian leaders, having New England connections, were typically moderate antislavery types, while the Old School sided with the theologically conservative South in wanting to sidestep this and other social reform issues.

"Old School" and "New School" outlooks had thus emerged as the two leading American patterns of being Reformed. The Old School was most characteristically doctrinalist, while the more innovative New School combined pietist revivalism with a culturalist emphasis, inherited from the Puritans, looking for a Christianization of American life. These divisions were not confined to Presbyterians, although they took their clearest shape among them. A number of smaller denominations, including some Baptists, were strictly Reformed doctrinalist groups. Other groups, among whom were some Baptists, the Reformed Church in America, and especially the majority of New England's Congregationalists, were clearly in the New School camp and part of the Reformed wing of the formidable American evangelical coalition that stressed pietism and culturalism. Through the Civil War era, these two schools of Reformed were not irreconcilable, especially once the slavery issue was removed. Most notably, after the war, in 1869 the New School and Old School Presbyterians in the North reunited.

The South, on the other hand, remained separate, holding on to its predominantly Old School tradition and urging the church to stay out of politics. Ironically this apolitical stance of the southern church was deeply mixed with defense of the southern way of life. Accordingly, during the next century the Old School doctrinalism of the Southern Presbyterians was associated with (at least local) cultural influence. In the North, on the other hand, confessionalism lost much of its social base and became more and more associated with a remnant mentality.

The New School heritage, on the other hand, emerged by the end of the century as the stronger of the two traditions in the North. The New School, however, was a combination of two emphases, pietist and culturalist, and these were separable. The divorce between them occurred under the pressures associated with the rapid modernization and secularization of American life between 1870 and 1930. Industrialization, urbanization, immigration, and pluralization undermined the social basis for the old evangelical (and often Reformed) religious quasi-establishment. Moreover, liberal democratic ideology, emphasizing human freedom, ability, and essential goodness, undermined the distinctly Calvinist doctrines. Even more basically, the new naturalistic science and history of the day challenged the authority of the Bible.

Broadly considered, evangelical Christians who responded to these crises moved in one of two directions. One group adjusted to modern times by toning down the supernaturalistic aspects of the gospel and stressing rather those parts of the Christian message that could be realized by developing natural (although God-given) human individual or cultural potentials. On the other side, conservatives reemphasized the fundamentals of the faith, which stressed God's supernatural interventions into history. Thus in the Reformed communities, as in many other areas of American life, a new division was superimposed on existing patterns.

The modernist accommodations to prevailing ideas and ideals fit least well with doctrinalist emphases and best with culturalist. Such theological liberalism was in principle compatible with some pietist emphases (as in a romantic religion of the heart), but in the long run piety proved difficult to sustain from generation to generation without a strong sense of radical divine intervention.

In the New School traditions (including Presbyterian, Congregationalist, Reformed Church in America, Baptist, and other heirs of the nineteenth-century evangelical mainstream), where doctrinalism was not especially strong, the new liberalism flourished, at least among some of the denominational leadership. It grew first, in the late Victorian era, as a version of evangelical romantic piety. In the progressive era, following the turn of the century, it also blossomed as part of the theological basis for the social gospel movement. By this time liberal Protestantism was moving away from crucial parts of traditional evangelical doctrine, repudiating emphases on personal salvation through trust in Christ's work of substitutionary atonement and rejecting the infallibility and reliability of Scripture. These liberal notions alarmed some of the heirs to revivalist pietism. Ecclesiastical warfare broke out and eventually brought a long series of splits between the two camps. Since the social gospel was associated with the modernist tendencies, the "fundamentalist" opponents tended to reject all "social gospels," or culturalist emphases. Such rejections, however, were seldom consistently sustained. New School revivalists also had a heritage of aspiring to Christianize America on a voluntary basis. Thus even when, especially after about 1920, fundamentalists decried the social gospel, they typically still endorsed a politically conservative culturalism that involved efforts to return America to nineteenth-century evangelical standards, as was seen in the anti-evolution and prohibition movements.

The supernaturalist or fundamentalist party among the Reformed included major elements of Old School or doctrinalist heritage as well as the successors to New School evangelicalism. The Old School party, centered first at Princeton Theological Seminary and after 1929 at Westminster Theological Seminary, provided intellectual foundations for defending the traditional faith. The common enemy, modernism, brought these strict confessionalists into close alliance with Reformed people of more New School or pietist-revivalist heritage for a time. Thus by the early 1930s the strictly confessionalist Presbyterians who followed New Testament scholar and apologist J. Gresham Machen were closely allied with Presbyterians among the more strictly revivalist fundamentalists, such as those at Wheaton College or Moody Bible Institute.

The groupings among these theologically Reformed fundamentalists were complicated by the presence of still another major new camp—the dispensationalists. Dispensationalism was essentially Reformed in its nineteenth-century origins and had in later nineteenth-century America spread most among revival-oriented Calvinists. Strict Old School confessionalists were, however, uneasy with dispensationalists' separation of the Old Testament dispensation of Law from the era of Grace in the church age. Dispensationalism, accordingly, was accepted most readily by Reformed Christians who had a more New School, or revivalist-evangelical, emphasis than among the various Old School, or doctrinalist, groups. During the fundamentalist controversies, however, these two groups were thrown into each other's arms.

The union, however, did not last. In 1937 the followers of Machen who had just left the Presbyterian Church in the U.S.A. split roughly into Old School and New School camps, with the more revivalist group, led by Carl McIntire, favoring dispensationalism and total abstinence from alcoholic beverages. About the same time, doctrinalist Southern Presbyerians took a stand against dispensationalism in their denomination.

Another, less separatist branch of the New School evangelical party survived well in the "new evangelicalism" that grew out of fundamentalism after World War II. The new evangelicals were largely Reformed in leadership and had moved away from strict dispensationalism. Institutionally they gained strength at centers such as Wheaton College, Fuller Theological Seminary, Trinity Evangelical Divinity School, and Gordon-Conwell Theological Seminary. *Christianity Today*, founded in 1956 under the editorship of Carl F. H. Henry, gave them wide visibility and influence. Inter-Varsity Christian Fellowship, InterVarsity Press, and the ministry of Francis Schaeffer also added substantially to the outreach of this Reformed evangelicalism. Keeping cordial relations with many individuals and groups not Reformed and with evangelicals both within and outside mainline denominations, this New School tradition has emerged as one of the most influential expressions of evangelicalism today.

The Old School, though smaller, also remains active. It has wide influence through Westminster Theological Seminary and similar conservative schools. Denominationally, it is especially strong in the Presbyterian Church of America and in the conservative wing of the Christian Reformed Church. It is also found among Reformed Baptists and in other smaller Reformed denominations.

Of the three strands of the heritage, the culturalist emphasis is the least unified today. Nonetheless, it is perhaps as prominent as it ever has been. This continuing emphasis, that Calvinists should be transforming culture and bringing all of creation back to its proper relationship to God's law, has been resurgent due to the convergence of a number of developments. Most clearly articulating these views have been the North American Kuyperians, followers of the turn-of-the-century Dutch theologian and politician, Abraham Kuyper. Kuyperianism was brought to America largely by the Dutch-American Christian Reformed Church, where a hard-line Kuyperianism also developed among the admirers of

Dutch philosopher Herman Dooyeweerd. Dooyeweerdianism has enlisted non-Dutch disciples, but the widest influence of Kuyperianism spread in a mild form through the neoevangelical movement after World War II. The fundamentalist tradition, said neoevangelical spokespersons such as Carl F. H. Henry, had not sufficiently recognized that the Christian task involves relating a Christian "World-and-life view" to all of culture and politics.[6]

By the 1970s such moderately conservative emphases were converging with the resurgence of conservative politics among American fundamentalists and fundamentalistic evangelicals. Fundamentalists had their own, vaguely Reformed, traditions of wanting to Christianize America. Versions of Kuyperian Calvinism such as those suggested by Francis Schaeffer in the influential political ministry of his later years helped articulate the new fundamentalist conservative political emphases of the Moral Majority. Schaeffer drew many of his political ideas from the work of the politically conservative Dooyeweerdian thinker, Rousas J. Rushdoony. Rushdoony also contributed to the emergence of the hyper-Reformed "theonomist" movement, which insists that Old Testament law should be the basis of American civil law.

The irony in this resurgence of Reformed culturalism is that the culturalists, who are often united in theological theory, are so deeply divided in practice. Cutting across the culturalist movement is a seemingly insurmountable divide between those who are politically conservative and those who are politically liberal. Many of the American followers of Kuyper have been politically liberal and these had an impact on the politically progressive evangelicalism that emerged during the 1960s and early 1970s.[7] Moreover, the politically liberal Reformed culturalist camp includes Reformed Christians in mainline denominations whose traditions still reflect the political progressivism of the social gospel days. In addition, the neoorthodox heritage in such denominations has contributed, especially via the work of H. Richard Niebuhr and Reinhold Niebuhr, to generally Reformed culturalist sensibilities tempered by a Lutheran sense of the ambiguities inherent in relating Christianity to an essentially pagan culture.

The American Reformed community today, then, still includes substantial representation of the three classic emphases, doctrinalism, pietism, and culturalism. These three are, of course, not incompatible and the unity of Reformed Christians in America would be much greater were this compatibility recognized and emphasized.

The question of unity, however, is complicated by the twentieth-century divisions of modernists and fundamentalists that have cut across the traditional divisions. Neoorthodox and dispensationalist variations add further complications. Moreover, among those who are primarily culturalists, conflicting political allegiances subvert Reformed unity. Nonetheless, there remain a substantial number of Reformed Christians whose faith reflects a balance, or potential balance, of the three traditional emphases. It is these Christians who need to find each other and who might benefit from reflecting on what it should mean to be Reformed.

They can also learn from considering the characteristic weaknesses, as well as the strengths, of their tradition. Perhaps the greatest fault of American Reformed communities since Puritan times is that they have cultivated an elitism. Ironically, the doctrine of election has been unwittingly construed as meaning that Reformed people have been endowed with superior theological, spiritual, or moral merit by God himself. The great irony of this is that the genius of the Reformed faith has been its uncompromising emphasis on God's grace, with the corollary that our own feeble efforts are accepted, not because of any merit, but solely due to God's grace and Christ's work. The doctrine of grace, then, ought to cultivate humility as a conspicuous trait of Reformed spirituality. A strong sense of our own inadequacies is an important asset for giving us positive appreciation of those who differ from us.

Yet too often Reformed people have been so totally confident of their own spiritual insights that they have been unable to accept or work with fellow Reformed Christians whose emphases may vary slightly. Perhaps some review of the rich varieties of theological views among the Reformed in America today will contribute to bringing tolerance and search for balance. Moreover, the unmistakable minority status of the "Reformed" in America today should help foster the need for mutual understanding and respect. Above all, however, a revival of the central Reformed distinctive—the sense of our own unworthiness and of total dependence on God's grace, as revealed especially through Christ's sacrificial work—should bring together many who in late twentieth-century America still find it meaningful to say "I am Reformed."

Notes: Reformed and American

1. I. John Hesselink, *On Being Reformed: Distinctive Characteristics and Common Misunderstandings* (Ann Arbor: Servant Books, 1983), 2 and 113.

2. This concept is elaborated in *Evangelicalism and Modern America*, ed. George M. Marsden (Grand Rapids: Wm. B. Eerdmans Publishing Company, 1984).

3. These categories are roughly those suggested by Nicholas Wolterstorff, "The AACS in the CRC," *The Reformed Journal* 24 (December 1974): 9-16.

4. Harry S. Stout, *The New England Soul: Preaching and Religious Culture in Colonial New England* (New York: Oxford University Press, forthcoming).

5. The Reformed efforts to build a Christian culture are well described in Fred J. Hood, *Reformed America: The Middle and Southern States, 1783-1837* (University, AL: University of Alabama Press, 1980).

6. Carl F. H. Henry, *The Uneasy Conscience of Modern Fundamentalism* (Grand Rapids: Wm. B. Eerdmans Publishing Company, 1947), 10.

7. See Robert Booth Fowler, *A New Engagement: Evangelical Political Thought, 1966-1976* (Grand Rapids: Wm. B. Eerdmans Publishing Company, 1982), for an account of this relationship and other developments in evangelical political thought.

1

THE SOUTHERN TRADITION

MORTON SMITH

THERE are several distinctively southern developments of Reformed thought in America. The Reformed faith is found primarily in the mainline Presbyterian Church, though it should be recognized that other branches of the Church in the South have held to the Reformed Faith to a greater or lesser degree. The Associate Reformed Presbyterian Church, for example, still maintains the Reformed faith as set forth in the Westminster standards. The Cumberland Presbyterians have rejected the doctrines of full predestination, and thus hold only a corrupted form of them. Various Baptist groups hold to elements of the Reformed faith. Taking Warfield's basic premise, that all true Christians hold to Reformed faith wherever they are true to the Word, one could also say that all evangelical churches in the South hold elements of the Reformed faith.

The South was greatly affected by the revival movements of the past two centuries. One of the results of these revival movements was the development of the common consensus on the Christian religion that marked the "Bible Belt." The basic elements of this consensus are an acceptance of the Bible as God's Holy Word, the recognition of our sinful and lost condition, and the conviction that the only way of salvation is to be found in Christ, who is to be received by faith. Insofar as these are all points that the Reformed faith teaches, it may be said that this much of the faith is held by the vast majority of all evangelical churches in the South. This same revivalism, on the other hand, with its strong emphasis on human ability to respond to gospel invitations, tended to minimize or even deny the Reformed distinctives, such as the doctrines of election, definite atonement, and efficacious grace.

Presbyterianism in the Colonial Period

Because the main developments in Reformed thought occurred in the Presbyterian Church, we shall concentrate on this church. The history of Presbyterianism in the South extends back to the first permanent settlement in Virginia in 1607. Ernest Trice Thompson in his *Presbyterians in the South* indicates that during the Colonial period there was no "South," but three different societies in the southern colonies: the Chesapeake society, based on tobacco; the Carolina society, built on rice and indigo; and finally the Back Country, still in the process of formation at the time of the Revolution.[1]

The Chesapeake society was the oldest. The Virginia Company's charter prescribed that "the word and services of God be preached, planted and used according to the rites and doctrines of the Church of England." The control of the Company was in the hands of the Puritans until the revocation of the charter in 1624. With the assumption of royal control of the colony in 1624, an act of conformity was passed. During the 1640s, despite Puritan control of Parliament in England, Governor William Berkeley continued to enforce conformity to the Church of England. This resulted in the departure of a number of colonists to Maryland at the invitation of Governor William Stone. They settled in Anne Arundel, Charles, and Prince George counties, near the present city of Annapolis. It is of interest that the ancestors of B. B. Warfield, one of America's greatest Presbyterian theologians, came to this region during this time.

During the period of the Commonwealth in England, the Puritans of Virginia were unmolested. A number of Scottish settlers arrived during the seventeenth century and settled along the Elizabeth River, near present-day Norfolk. Others settled along the Rappahannock, James, and Potomac Rivers.

Francis Makemie's main labors were on the eastern shore of Virginia and Maryland. He is sometimes known as the father of American Presbyterianism because of his leadership in organizing the first presbytery in the colonies. This was the Presbytery of Philadelphia, founded in 1705 or 1706. It had a very small beginning. There were four ministers from Maryland, two from Delaware, and one from Philadelphia.

Further South, there was a settlement of Presbyterians around Charleston, South Carolina, which had no relationship with the Presbytery of Philadelphia. The earliest records of Reformed worship in that area are of the French Huguenots. The last will and testament of a certain Caesar Mozé reveals that there must have been a French church in the Charleston area as early as 1687. There were also a goodly number of Scots, Dutch, and New England Puritans in South Carolina. An independent church, sometimes called Presbyterian, was formed in Charleston about 1690. It was composed of various peoples: French, Scots, Scotch-Irish, and New Englanders. A whole colony of New Englanders moved to South Carolina to found a Congregational church at Dorchester in

1696. Between 1752 and 1771 much of this group transplanted itself to Liberty County, Georgia, and established Midway Church there. From this Congregational church a large number of young men were fed into the ministry of various denominations. The Presbyterians received some 30, including Thomas Goulding, first professor at Columbia Seminary, and Daniel Baker, the great Presbyterian evangelist to the old Southwest. An independent Scottish Church was established in Savannah, Georgia, which still exists as the Independent Presbyterian Church of Savannah. Its grant of land from George II states that it is to be used for such "as are or shall be professors of the Doctrines of the Church of Scotland, agreeable to the Confession of Faith. . . ."[2]

An independent presbytery developed in the Charleston area, which George Howe, historian of the Presbyterian Church in South Carolina to 1850, dates from 1728. This presbytery required subscription to the *Westminster Confession of Faith*, as indicated in correspondence regarding the Rev. Josiah Smith, who was excluded in 1730 because of his refusal to subscribe. This presbytery passed out of existence at the time of the Revolution.

The independence of spirit reflected in the Charleston-Savannah area has been characteristic of much southern thought. No doubt it was forced on the early Presbyterians of this southern region simply by their distance from the rest of the American Presbyterians, but it was to leave a mark on the South Carolina Presbyterian mind. The people of this same area disagreed with their brethren in 1837-38 and formed the Independent Presbyterian denomination, which went its own way until the War between the States overshadowed their differences and brought about a union with other Southern Presbyterians.

The mainline Synod of the Presbyterian Church in 1729 adopted the *Westminster Confession* and *Catechisms* as the confession of faith of the Synod. Having thus declared herself, the Church might be assumed to have embarked on smooth sailing, but such was not the case. A controversy arose that was to divide the Church in 1741 between the Old Side Synod of Philadelphia and what later became the New Side Synod of New York. This division occurred in part as a result of the great revivals of George Whitefield and his followers and the development of the "log colleges" and academies for the training of ministers. The New Side, which espoused the revivals and the use of the academies, planted a number of churches in Virginia.

The Blairs maintained an Academy at Fagg's Manor, Chester County, Pennsylvania, at which Samuel Davies was to be educated. Davies may properly be called the "Father of Southern Presbyterianism" since his labors brought about the establishment of the Mother Presbytery of the South, namely, Hanover Presbytery. He labored off and on in Virginia from 1747 to 1759, and convened the first meeting of the Presbytery of Hanover on December 3, 1755, at the direction of the Synod of New York. The effects of his ministry were felt over all of Virginia and North Carolina. He held the *Westminster Confession* and *Catechisms* in the highest esteem. It was his regular practice to teach the *Shorter Catechism* to all of his members, and to have it recited at the worship service on Sunday.

William Henry Foote, writing a century later, in 1850, speaks of John Robinson and Samuel Davies and of their teachers, the Tennents and the Blairs, as laying a foundation that "had a controlling influence over Virginia Presbyterians in creed and practice" to his day. He says:

> From the time of these men, the Virginia ministers and people have believed in awakenings,—in spiritual exercises in religion,—in the power of godliness in men's hearts and lives. From deep conviction they have been believers in the depravity of human nature,—the sovereignty of God,—original sin,—and the absolute necessity of the new birth. Hoping for justification by the righteousness of Christ made theirs by faith, believing it would be safe to appear in it, in the judgment to come, ministers and people rejoiced in the unsearchable riches of Christ, through trials and difficulties that would make ordinary spirits tremble and quit the field. By the help of God they have left us a good report.[3]

In 1746 John Blair organized churches at North Mountain, New Providence, Timber Ridge, and the Fork of the James; these became the nucleus of Lexington Presbytery. It was out of the New Providence and Timber Ridge Churches that Liberty Hall Academy, the predecessor of Washington College (now Washington and Lee University), was to come. William Graham was the first teacher at the academy. He taught Archibald Alexander, the founding professor of Princeton Seminary. Others who came from this school were Moses Hoge, John Holt Rice, and George Addison Baxter. Hoge was the first professor of theology, appointed by the Synod of Virginia. Rice succeeded him, and founded Union Seminary. Baxter was professor of theology there at the time of the Old School–New School division of 1837.

Despite the fact that the Presbyterian Church of the South was marked with the revivalism of the New Side, there was a failure to follow up the gains of the first awakening. One of the major problems lay in the requirement of the Presbyterian Church for a highly educated ministry. There was a dearth of institutions in the South for such preparation. The Baptists and Methodists, on the other hand, had no such requirement. They used the itinerant system and the revivalism of Whitefield to reach the masses, and thus many who otherwise would have been Presbyterians were taken over into these groups. Even as

Presbyterians became established in the Southland and set up schools and academies, they were not able to keep pace with the demand for ministers during this period. It is hard to see how it would have been possible to have met the demands of the day with the limited resources that were available. Whether a plan could have been worked out and executed to meet the needs or not, it must be admitted that the Presbyterians failed to work out such a plan.

Presbyterianism After the Revolution

The period of the Revolution and following was marked by skepticism and widespread immorality. Especially was this true on the frontier. God graciously sent a revival of religion during this era, however. As early as 1787 an awakening began at Hampden-Sydney College in Prince Edward County, Virginia, that was to affect Presbyterianism for future generations because of those brought under its influence. It was a movement that enjoyed the participation of the President of the College, John Blair Smith. It spread to the sister institution of the Presbyterians across the Blue Ridge, Liberty Hall Academy, where William Graham participated in it. Through these two institutions the future leadership of the Presbyterian Church was affected. Archibald Alexander gave his heart to Christ under its influence. This young man was to become one of the country's greatest theologians. He received his theological education from William Graham. In 1812 he was called by the General Assembly to found Princeton Seminary. He was to serve there until his death in 1851. Charles Hodge was one of his students and became his colleague on the faculty. He taught a theology that was to become known as "Princeton Theology." Herman Bavinck described this theology thus: "The so-called Princeton Theology is chiefly a reproduction of the Calvinism of the seventeenth century, as it is formulated in the *Westminster Confession* and the *Consensus Helveticus*, and especially elucidated by F. Turretin in his *Theologia Elenctica*."[4] One may well question whether it should be called "Princeton" since it was taken from Virginia to Princeton by Alexander. Bavinck is correct in identifying this theology with that of Turretin. His work was used as the textbook on theology at both Princeton and Union Seminaries prior to the publication of Hodge's *Systematic Theology* at Princeton and Dabney's *Lectures in Systematic Theology* at Union.

Others to be affected by the revival in Virginia were Moses Hoge, John Holt Rice, George Addison Baxter, and Drury Lacy, all of whom helped to shape the theology of Virginia Presbyterianism. Moses Hoge was the President of Hampden-Sydney and the first officially appointed teacher of theology of the Synod of Virginia. John Holt Rice was to become the founder of Union Theological Seminary, and George Addison Baxter to succeed him there as Professor of Theology. Through these men the following generations received their training in the same sort of Presbyterianism that Alexander had carried to Princeton from Virginia. The affinity of Union and Princeton can be seen in a letter written by Rice to Alexander concerning his own hopes for his newly formed seminary:

> If, however, a Seminary can be established in the South, many will frequent it, who will not go to the North. . . . But my plan is, if we can succeed here, to take Princeton as our model, to hold constant correspondence with that great and most valuable institution, to get the most promising of our young men to finish off at Princeton; and, in a word, as far as possible, make this a sort of branch of that, so as to have your spirit diffused through us, and do all that can be done to bind the different parts of the Church together.[5]

That such a close relationship continued to exist is a matter of historical record. It may be seen in a number of ways. For one thing, both of these institutions were associated with the Old School branch of the Church in 1837 and following. Robert L. Dabney of Union Seminary received a call to Princeton in 1860. Again in 1915 Union Seminary sought to obtain the services of J. Gresham Machen of Princeton in New Testament. As recently as 1930-1940 Union Seminary had a Systematic Theology professor, James Porter Smith, who taught the same theology as that set forth at Princeton. The testimony of Smith's brother-in-law, the Rev. Gaston Boyle, is to this effect: "I am positive that he believed and taught the system of theology taught by Hodge and Dabney, including their beliefs concerning election, predestination and the inspiration of the Scriptures."[6] Thus the same theology that was taken by Alexander from Virginia and planted at Princeton continued to be the theology both of Princeton Seminary and of Union Seminary in Virginia for at least a century.

The Hampden-Sydney revival was to have far-reaching effects on the frontier, for through it James McGready was influenced to enter into evangelistic efforts in North Carolina. Thus the revival spread to Guilford and Orange Counties in 1791. McGready had a number of other ministers associated with him in his revival efforts, and moved into Kentucky. In 1798 McGready drew up a covenant with others to pray for one year for a revival. In answer to their prayer the revival began with the semi-annual sacramental service celebrated in July 1799 at Red River. The following year saw an increase of the revival in Cumberland County. McGready initiated the camp meeting that was to become characteristic of the Great Revival. He invited people to come prepared to camp for a sacramental season at Gasper River.

The Great Revival was a mixed blessing. On the one hand, many were brought to confess Christ as Savior. On the other hand, it led to the excesses for which the Kentucky revivals became known, namely, jerking, rolling, running, dancing, and barking. Not all the ministers countenanced such exercises, though some encouraged them and thus encouraged confusion. A worse side-effect of the revivals was the fact that there arose an uneducated ministry in Kentucky that, because of lack of training in the Scriptures and the standards of the church, began preaching and teaching something less than the full gospel of sovereign grace. A number of young men were licensed or ordained in the newly formed Cumberland Presbytery without having to subscribe to the *Confession of Faith,* except so far as they believed it to agree with the Word of God. Some rejected in particular the "alleged fatalism" of the Confession, which they thought the doctrines of predestination and reprobation implied. When, in response to complaint, the Synod of Kentucky investigated the irregularities and called for those licensed and ordained under such procedure to be reexamined, they refused to obey. The following year the Synod dissolved the Presbytery. Those who were unwilling to submit to the Synod withdrew and established a new and independent Cumberland Presbytery in 1810. Changes were made in the *Westminster Confession* by this group. Schaff summarizes the effect of their change: "The Cumberland Confession teaches on the one hand conditional election and unlimited atonement, and on the other, the final perseverance of the saints. It is an eclectic compromise between Calvinism and Arminianism; it is half Calvinistic and half Arminian, and makes no attempt to harmonize these antagonistic elements."[7]

In addition to the Cumberland Schism of 1810 there was another schism in the Upper Kentucky region led by Barton Stone. This movement was particularly anticonfessional. It arose because of the objection by more orthodox Presbyterians to the Arminianism of some of the revivalists. They in turn assumed that the creedal subscription of Presbyterianism was antievangelistic, and renounced creedal subscription. There was first an attempt to form an independent Presbytery of Springfield, which would be a part of the Presbyterian Church but not under the Synod of Kentucky. This Presbytery lasted just nine months during 1803-04. Some of its members were drawn away into the Shaker groups, while Barton Stone, rejecting all denominationalism, founded the so-called "Christian Church." In 1832 this body was to become associated with the group started by Thomas and Alexander Campbell under the name "Disciples of Christ." This movement continues in the South under the name "The Church of Christ" as well as the Christian Church. Sad to say, the "Church of Christ" has departed from the doctrine of justification by faith alone of the Protestant Reformation. They hold to a faith-plus-works doctrine, including the necessity of water baptism for salvation.

Despite the loss of the Cumberland and Disciples groups and the confusion caused by the excesses of the Great Revival, this movement did greatly affect the moral life of the country. Hays says, "Religion, from being a mere matter of contempt on the part of public men, became an essential and influential part of the general public sentiment of the Country."[8]

Generally speaking, only a few Presbyterian ministers were involved in these reactions to the full Calvinism of the Reformed faith. One of the basic problems in both the Cumberland and Disciples divisions was a lack of proper education of the revivalists and ministers ordained in Kentucky. This serves to confirm the historic position of the Presbyterian Church of insisting on a well-educated ministry, for it is all too easy to deviate from the full counsel of God if one has not been properly trained in handling the Word of Truth.

While the South was faced with the deviations brought on by revivalism, the Presbyterian Church in the North was involved in a plan to settle the newly opened Middle West that allowed New England Congregationalists to enter the Presbyterian Church without subscribing to the Westminster standards. Hopkinsian theology was on the rise in New England at this time. This meant that many of the Congregationalists who joined the Presbyterian Church came with a theology that was not Reformed. This became known as New School Theology.

By and large the Presbyterian Church in the South was not affected by New School Theology. There was a consciousness in the South of the fact that there was a difference between the Church North and South. This gave rise to the concept of "our Southern Zion" as early as the 1820s. The southern mind-set of simple trust in the Bible tended to cause a reaction against theological debate on matters that were not as clear as the basic evangelical tenets. The South remained generally aloof from the Old School–New School controversy. It was only with the clear deviation by the 1836 Assembly from the historic Reformed faith that Southerners became aroused.

Thompson says: "The Southern presbyteries, holding the balance of power in the Assembly, were generally in favor of ecclesiastical boards rather than the independent and co-operative Societies, and were overwhelmingly staunch in their adherence to the Westminster Standards and thus opposed to the New School 'heresies.' "[9]

Only in east Tennessee, where there was a breakdown of church discipline, was a college established where the Hopkinsian errors were taught. It is difficult to understand the failure of the Church to exercise discipline here, except that the founder of Abingdon Presbytery and the president of Greeneville College was the one who introduced these views. There was a natural hesitancy on the part of men more recently come to the presbytery and of some who had been educated under Mr. Balch to bring a charge against him. Also, the seriousness of Hopkinsian views was not fully recognized, especially in the light of the fact that Balch affirmed his belief in the *Confession* whenever brought before a court. A basic lesson to be learned is that personalities or position should not be allowed to prevent the proper exercise of discipline. Had the 1837 division not come when it did, a great deal more of the New School theology might have developed in the South than actually did develop.

It is interesting to observe that the few Southern Presbyterians who united with the New School Assembly did so for other than doctrinal reasons. Only in Tennessee, where, as we have already seen, the New School theology had a foothold, was there a majority of New School adherents. Even here it was not really because of theological agreement with the New School that these adhered to the New School Assembly. Rather, this may be accounted for by the influence of Hezekiah Balch, and by the fact that this area had been largely dependent on the American Home Missionary Society and the American Educational Society, both based in New England, for financial support. J. E. Alexander, historian of the Synod, says, "Though doctrinal differences constituted one of the causes of the division, it was evidently only a small portion of the Presbyterian ministers of the New School Body who held the doctrines of the New Divinity, at least in their full extent. The great majority of them were no doubt strictly orthodox and were influenced by the other considerations already mentioned."[10] The record of the Synod states the grounds as "the unconstitutional and unrighteous acts" of the two Reforming Assemblies, without mentioning doctrinal grounds.

In most of the other Synods minorities went independent, as in the case of the minority of the Presbytery of Charleston-Union and the Presbytery of Etowah in Georgia, which joined the New School Church. (The Charleston-Union Presbytery rejoined the Old School in 1852, and the Etowah Presbytery disappeared a few years after its formation.) In general, these defections from the Old School Church were not on theological grounds. The fear that the New School group would eventually denounce slavery as unchristian was appealed to by some as a ground for going with the Old School. On the other hand, the fear of centralization of power as represented by the 1837 exscinding action of the General Assembly was the motivation for some in Mississippi and South Carolina to withdraw from the Old School Assembly. Many felt that the actions of the 1837 Assembly had been unconstitutional, and thus allied themselves with the New School. Thompson concludes that "New School support in the South, with the possible exception of eastern Tennessee, was based overwhelmingly on opposition to what seemed unauthorized and unconstitutional authority exercised by the two Reforming Assemblies."[11]

Distinctive Theological Emphases

The Southern Presbyterian Church was essentially Old School in character. It is well to see what was peculiar to this brand of Presbyterianism. First, it was marked by strict subscription to the Westminster standards as the confession and constitution of the Church. Being thus committed to the Westminster standards, it was a Calvinistic church, embracing all of the tenets that go under that name.

The historic Puritan and Scottish doctrine of the sole headship of Christ over his church was maintained. Out of this came the high view of the church, that it is a positive institution of Christ and must do only what he teaches it to do in his Word. Thornwell of South Carolina was to carry out this principle with the greatest consistency, opposing at points such men as Charles Hodge of Princeton on certain matters of polity. Though Thornwell did not carry the day in the undivided church, his views were to prevail in the Southern Church after 1861.

Thornwell maintained that the church "is a positive institution, and therefore must show a definite warrant for everything that she does. It is not enough that her measures are not condemned, they must be sanctioned, positively sanctioned, by the power which ordains her, or they are null and void."[12] He opposed the use of boards to carry out the work of the church. Rather, the church courts ought to handle this directly. Instead of an independent, or semi-independent, board carrying on the work of missions the General Assembly should carry this work on through committees directly responsible to the Assembly. This position was adopted by the Southern Presbyterian Church, and though it abandoned it in the 1940s, the Presbyterian Church in America, which separated from the Southern Church in 1973, has returned to it.

A distinctively southern view of the office of the ruling elder arose. Following the 1837-38 division the practice of having the ruling elder lay hands on a man being ordained to the office of the ministry began in Kentucky. The General Assembly of 1843 declared that "neither the Constitution nor the practice of our Church authorizes Ruling Elders to impose hands in the ordination of ministers."[13] Drs. R. J. Breckinridge and J. H. Thornwell took issue with this double ruling of the Assembly. They maintained that the New Testament elder included both teaching and ruling elders, that as true elders they were an integral element of a presbytery and thus necessary to its regular constitution, and that they had a right to participate in all of the actions of presbytery including all steps to the ordination of ministers. The Assembly, however, in 1844 followed Hodge in denying the necessity of ruling elders in presbytery, and their right to participate in the ordination of ministers. With the division of 1861 the view of Thornwell became the accepted view of the Southern Presbyterian Church and continues to be one of the distinctives of this Church.[14] This has also been carried over into the Presbyterian Church in America.

Another southern development in church polity was the idea that the office of deacon is to handle all the temporal affairs of the church. This was first enunciated by Thomas Smythe of Charleston, South Carolina. The idea of systematic benevolences was also developed during this period, and had the support of such Southerners as Stuart Robinson and J. H. Thornwell. Generally speaking, the southern leaders of this period opposed instrumental music and liturgical elements in the worship service. This, of course, grows out of the *jure divino* view of church polity and worship that was held in the South.

This same view of the church was applied to the burning social issue of slavery:

> The Church of Christ is a spiritual body, whose jurisdiction extends only to the religious faith and moral conduct of her members. She cannot legislate where Christ has not legislated, nor make terms of membership which He has not made. . . .
>
> Since Christ and his inspired Apostles did not make the holding of slaves a bar to communion, we, as a court of Christ, have no authority to do so; since they did not attempt to remove it from the Church by legislation, we have no authority to legislate on the subject.[15]

This view of the church, which prevented the Assembly from legislating on the issue of slavery, kept the Old School body intact until 1861. Only then, under the heat of the circumstances of war, did the Assembly break with this principle and pass the Gardiner Spring Resolution. This resolution in effect decided the political issue between the North and South, and virtually exscinded all Southern Presbyterians from the Church. It said:

> Resolved, . . . that this General Assembly . . . do hereby acknowledge and declare our obligations to promote and perpetuate, so far as in us lies, the integrity of these United States, and to strengthen, uphold, and encourage the Federal Government in the exercise of all its functions under our noble Constitution; and to this Constitution in all its provisions, requirements, and principles, we profess our unabated loyalty. . . .[16]

Charles Hodge of Princeton, with 57 others, protested this action of the Assembly. This protest states in part: "The General Assembly in thus deciding a political question, and in making that decision practically a condition of membership to the Church, has, in our judgment, violated the Constitution of the Church, and usurped the prerogative of its Divine Master."[17]

B. M. Palmer, first Moderator of the Southern Assembly, declared:

> This question, lying wholly within the domain of politics, the General Assembly assumed the right to determine; so that, even if not ejected by what was equivalent to an act of expulsion, the Southern Presbyteries were compelled to separate themselves, in order to preserve the crown rights of the Redeemer and the spiritual independence of His kingdom and the Church. . . .[18]

The Presbyteries of the South dissolved their connection with the General Assembly of the Presbyterian Church in the United States of America. A total of 47 Presbyteries, making up 10 Synods, thus withdrew. On the 4th of December, 1861, at the First Presbyterian Church of Augusta, Georgia, the commissioners from these Presbyteries met and constituted the first General Assembly of the Presbyterian Church in the Confederate States of America. This meeting was opened with a stirring sermon on the Kingship of Christ over His Church by B. M. Palmer, pastor of the First Presbyterian Church of New Orleans. After adopting its official name, the Assembly then formally adopted the Westminster standards as its constitution, thus continuing the American Presbyterian tradition of commitment to these doctrinal standards. That the Southern Presbyterian Church saw itself as a distinctively Old School Presbyterian Church may be seen in the fact that she spoke out most clearly against the way in which the Old and New School branches of the Northern church reunited in 1869, which she judged to be a total abandonment of the Old School heritage.[19]

The Southern Presbyterian Church was marked by certain distinctive characteristics during the first 75 years of its life. They were a commitment to the Bible as the inspired and infallible Word of God; a thoroughgoing and enthusiastic Calvinism, regarded as a part of the gospel that was to be preached to the people; and a view of the mission of the church as spiritual, which was maintained both in theory and in practice. She developed an ecclesiastical polity that was distinguished for its constitutionality, particularly as seen in the complete parity of the ruling elders with the teaching elders, the carefully defined spheres and rights of the several courts, and its opposition to centralism. She stood for a strict construction of and adherence to the Westminster standards both in theory and in practice.

The newborn Church was especially interested in missions as the supreme work of the church. Among the resolutions of that first Assembly regarding missions is this classic statement regarding the place of missionary work in the life of the church:

> Finally, the General Assembly desires distinctly and deliberately to inscribe on our church's banner, as she now unfurls it to the world, in immediate connection with the headship of our Lord, his last command: "Go ye into all the world and preach the gospel to every creature"; regarding this as the great end of her organization, and obedience to it as the indispensable condition of her Lord's promised presence, and as one great comprehensive object, a proper conception of whose vast magnitude and grandeur is the only thing which, in connection with the love of Christ, can ever sufficiently arouse her energies and develop her resources so as to cause her to carry on, with the vigor and efficiency which true fealty to her Lord demands, those other agencies necessary to her internal growth and home prosperity.[20]

A particular development in Southern Presbyterian theological thought should be noted. It was the development of the doctrine of adoption as a separate *locus* in the Columbia Seminary school of thought. Hodge and Dabney had followed Turretin and dealt with adoption in connection with justification. The Columbia theologians followed the *Confession* and *Catechisms*, and thus developed the doctrine of adoption as a separate *locus*. This line of thinking began with John L. Girardeau of Columbia, and was continued by R. A. Webb, his son-in-law, who taught at Louisville Seminary. He produced a work entitled *The Reformed Doctrine of Adoption*, which was printed after his death.

Prior to the War between the States, the southern way of life allowed time for the development of a deep scholarship. Men such as Alexander, Thornwell, Dabney, Warfield, and Machen were all products of the South. They are among the most distinguished theologians America has produced. After the War, and during the long course of the slow recovery of the South from the cultural upheaval that her defeat brought, relatively few scholars arose from the South. The result is that though the seminaries of the South remained essentially sound up to the 1930s and 1940s, they were not really producing deep thinkers. Orthodoxy began to be looked upon as unscholarly. In the meantime Presbyterians of the North drifted into liberalism. Thus, when Southerners went north for theological training they were exposed to liberalism, even at Princeton after Machen's departure in 1929. These men came back to teach at the southern seminaries. Their appeal to the rising young generation was that scholarship was on the liberal side. The result was a rapid decline of the Southern Presbyterian Church into liberalism. The last

General Assembly controlled by the conservative element in the Southern Presbyterian Church was in 1939. Since that time the orthodox Christian has had a constant struggle to maintain his position in the Southern Presbyterian Church.

Recent Developments

There was a group that saw the necessity of reforming their Church. They developed several different means of reform. First, the *Southern Presbyterian Journal* (now the *Presbyterian Journal*) became a rallying point for conservatives in the Church. The *Journal* had its beginnings in the late 1940s. Unsuccessful efforts were launched by students of Columbia Theological Seminary during the early 1950s to have a liberal professor removed. A number of these men are now in the leadership of the Presbyterian Church in America. Successful efforts were launched to keep some of the presbyteries and synods of the deep South conservative. Belhaven College became a coeducational institution in 1954, and soon began training a stream of pre-ministerial students who became convinced of the Reformed faith and maintained their convictions even though many attended the liberal seminaries of the denomination. A number of these men now constitute a significant element of the ministers of the Presbyterian Church in America. In addition to this, the Pensacola Theological Institute began to bring in Reformed scholars and preachers from all over the world. They trained not only theological students, but also a large number of laymen from across the South.

One of the most encouraging occurrences was the increasing number of conservative young men who were getting advanced degrees and returning to the South as strongly committed and well-trained defenders of the historic faith. Though committed to the basic Reformed faith that they had learned in the South, they brought with them insights from their various schools of study, thus enriching the theological thought of the South.

The outside institution that had the greatest influence on the conservative Southern Presbyterians was Westminster Theological Seminary. There are several reasons for this. One that has already been noted is the affinity that the Southern Presbyterians had with the Old Princeton theology. Westminster was, of course, the successor of Old Princeton. Second, a fair number of Southern Presbyterian ministers were educated at Westminster. The influence of these became particularly evident in the movement toward a new Church, since a number of these individuals became teachers.

In 1964 the foundations of the Reformed Theological Seminary of Jackson, Mississippi, were laid, and this seminary opened its doors in

1966. Though there was no actual formal relationship between Reformed Seminary and Westminster, the original faculty of Reformed Seminary, of which the present writer was a member, viewed it as something of a daughter seminary to Westminster. Several members of that faculty had been trained at Westminster. They certainly felt that the theology they were teaching was the same as that of Westminster, and thus they looked to Westminster for encouragement and aid. Several of the Westminster faculty, including Dr. Cornelius Van Til, visited Reformed Seminary and gave special lectures. The relation seems to have been similar to that which Union Seminary of Virginia had with Princeton in its early history.

Reformed Seminary became one of the primary sources for conservative ministers serving Presbyterianism in the South. At the beginning most of the graduates of the Seminary were placed in the more conservative presbyteries of the Presbyterian Church in the United States. Many of these were to identify with the Presbyterian Church in America when it was founded in 1973. Others remained in the Presbyterian Church in the United States (now merged with the Northern Church to form the PCUSA). Since the founding of the Presbyterian Church in America, the majority of the graduates of the Seminary have entered its ranks as ministers.

Since its founding, Reformed Theological Seminary has become the primary source of Reformed theological developments in the South. In what follows we shall review some of these developments. The Seminary has witnessed an interesting melding of a number of streams of Reformed thought. The majority of the faculty have been drawn out of the Southern Presbyterian background. These have stood largely in the tradition of Thornwell and Dabney. They have sought to maintain the historic Reformed faith as developed in Southern Presbyterianism, coupling a warmhearted evangelism with full commitment to the Reformed faith. One of the early areas of discussion at the Seminary was the question of how evangelism is to be carried out. Many of the students came to the Seminary with evangelistic methods that reflected an Arminian approach to man and not the Reformed view. Efforts were made to encourage men to think through more consistently the implications of the Reformed faith in the area of evangelism. Generally speaking, the Seminary encouraged the Evangelism Explosion methods developed at the Coral Ridge Presbyterian Church, Fort Lauderdale, Florida, to get people involved in personal evangelism. The present writer has written a pamphlet entitled "Reformed Evangelism" that has had a good reception.

A particular area where the influence of Westminster is seen is in the field of apologetics. Westminster Seminary departed from the Old Princeton theology in the study of apologetics as developed under the tutelage of Cornelius Van Til. Had Westminster Seminary not been formed in 1929 under the leadership of J. Gresham Machen, Dr. Van Til no doubt would have developed his thinking at Princeton, since he was already on the faculty there before Westminster began. The apologetics of Dr. Van Til has come to be known as presuppositional apologetics, as opposed to the traditional evidential apologetics of Old Princeton. American Presbyterianism in general had uncritically accepted the evidential approach to apologetics in its conflict with the deism of the eighteenth century. The present writer, who had some of his theological training at Westminster Seminary, taught both Systematic Theology and Apologetics at Reformed Seminary during its first decade. In theology, he followed the exegetical, biblical theological method of Professor John Murray. In apologetics he taught the presuppositional approach. A large number of Reformed graduates are thus committed to this view of theology and apologetics.

One of the interesting developments that took place at Reformed Seminary during this period was the brief professorship of Dr. Gregg Bahnsen in the field of apologetics and ethics. It was during this time that he published his book *Theonomy in Christian Ethics*. A number of his students became committed to reconstructionist postmillennialism and to theonomy. Though Dr. Bahnsen is no longer at Reformed Seminary, the impact of his instruction there is still felt in the South in that a small number of his followers are now in the ministry of the Presbyterian Church in America. Though the question of whether theonomy is acceptable in the Presbyterian Church in America has been raised, the Church has declined to get into this matter. It has indicated that theonomy should not become a test of orthodoxy. Not all have been pleased with this position, but they have permitted the coexistence in the Presbyterian Church in America of theonomists and nontheonomists.

Two groups of theonomists have left the PCA in order to have what they consider greater freedom in the propagation of their views. The first of these is the Westminster Presbyterian Church of Tyler, Texas. This Church operates a small theological school called Geneva, and produces a number of publications. Some of this Tyler group have renounced the time-honored "regulative principle" of worship of the Westminster Catechism of the Presbyterian Church, which states that we are to include in worship only what the Bible teaches. This group also espouses paedocommunion.

The other group that left the PCA over theonomy is a small group of churches headed by the Chalcedon Presbyterian Church of the Atlanta area. These churches have formed a small Presbyterian denomination known as the Reformed Presbyterian Church in the United States. This group has not displayed the same kinds of deviations from historic Presbyterianism that the Tyler group has shown. Both groups hold to reconstructionist postmillennialism.

A revival of postmillennialism as an acceptable eschatological view has occurred in Southern Presbyterianism during the past two decades. Though the majority of the ministers in the South hold to amillennialism, there are a large number of pre- and postmillennialists. Not all of the postmillennialists hold to the reconstructionist view of R. J. Rushdoony, but many hold to a more traditional postmillennialism.

Still another stream of thought that has entered Southern Presbyterian circles, largely through Westminster and Reformed Theological Seminaries, is the concept of a Christian world-and-life view. Abraham Kuyper's Stone Lectures on *Calvinism*, delivered at Princeton Theological Seminary in 1898, introduced this broad concept to the American Presbyterian world. Earlier American Presbyterians had practiced the idea of living their faith out in various areas of life, as may be seen from the fact that many of them were influential in early American political life. In the South, however, there had been something of a drawing back from it, due to a misapplication of Thornwell's doctrine of the spirituality of the church. Many Southern Presbyterians applied this to their personal lives as well as to the church. With the carefully thought-out ideas of Kuyper and his development of "sphere sovereignty" a more balanced view of how we are to view the application of Christian principles to every area of life, and not just to the church, was found. The theonomists, of course, embrace this concept, but so do many others who are not fully identified with theonomy. For example, the Christian Studies Center of Memphis, Tennessee, has been seeking to propagate the Kuyperian world-and-life view for a number of years through publications and lectures. This organization has been established and kept alive through the untiring labors of Robert Metcalf, a ruling elder of the Second Presbyterian Church of Memphis. The Christian Studies Center has not met with great success, but is cited here as an illustration of the breadth of Reformed thought that now exists in the South.

With the recognition of the stranglehold that the liberals had on all of the institutions and agencies of the Presbyterian Church in the United States, and with the beginning of groups departing from that Church, the leadership of the conservatives in the PCUS determined that there should be a separation from that Church in 1973. Generally speaking, an effort was put forth to make this as peaceable as possible. Churches and individuals simply notified their presbyteries of their intention to leave. The first General Assembly of the Presbyterian Church in America was held at Birmingham on December 4, 1973.

This body saw itself as continuing the historic Presbyterian faith that the Southern Presbyterian Church had held during its early years, and which it had in turn received from the Old School Presbyterian Church prior to that. The PCA may be called an Old School Presbyterian Church, holding to the inerrancy of the Scripture in the original autographs, strict subscription to the *Westminster Confession* and *Catechisms,* and to Southern Presbyterian Church polity.

This Church has from its beginning seen as its mission to reach across the whole nation, and not to remain a regional church as the Southern Presbyterian Church had done. In 1982 the Reformed Presbyterian Church, Evangelical Synod joined the PCA, accepting its Southern Presbyterian polity. Thus, this polity is now being practiced across the entire nation in this new and growing Church. The roots of the RPCES went back largely to the Old School segment of the Northern Church. It held to the Old Princeton theology. Thus in this "joining and receiving" the streams of "Southern" and "Princeton" theology again merged.

The Southern Presbyterian Church (PCUS) has united with the Northern Church (UPCUSA) to form the Presbyterian Church in the United States of America. There remain those who are sound in the faith in this Church, but by and large the denomination must be characterized as liberal in persuasion and direction. The distinctives of the earlier Southern Presbyterians have been lost in this body. These distinctives are now carried on in the Presbyterian Church in America, which encompasses both Canada and the United States.

In this essay we have traced some of the distinctive developments of Southern Presbyterian thought on the American church scene. We have seen that there has been a separate development in the past, but we have also noted that in this century a good deal of broadening has taken place. This seems to be in accord with what is presently happening to the South. Increasingly the South is becoming amalgamated with the rest of the country in its thought and culture. One wonders whether there will continue to be a distinctively Southern Presbyterian strand of theology, or whether it will not eventually be merged into the broad stream of Reformed thought found both in America and abroad. Should the Southern distinctives gradually be lost, some of the South's contributions will no doubt become a part of the larger whole, while the South itself will benefit from the many advances in Reformed thought that are taking place in other parts of the Lord's vineyard.

Notes: The Southern Tradition

1. Ernest Trice Thompson, *Presbyterians in the South,* vol. 1, *1607-1861* (Richmond, VA: John Knox Press, 1963), 629.

2. *History of the Independent Church and Sunday School, Savannah, Ga.* (Savannah: George N. Nichols, 1882).

3. William Henry Foote, *Sketches of Virginia: Historical and Biographical* (Philadelphia: n.p., 1850), 1:146.

4. Herman Bavinck, *Gereformeerde Dogmatiek*, 4th ed. (Kampen, J. H. Kok, 1928), 1:177.

5. John Holt Rice, Letter to Archibald Alexander, dated Richmond, March 5th, 1823, in William Maxwell, *A Memoir of the Rev. John H. Rice, D.D.* (Philadelphia and Richmond, VA: n.p., 1835), 233.

6. Letter from Gaston Boyle to Morton H. Smith, November 1961, in Morton Howison Smith, *Studies in Southern Presbyterian Theology* (Amsterdam: Van Campen, 1962), 320.

7. Philip Schaff, *Creeds of Christendom*, 4th ed. (New York: Harper and Brothers, 1919), 1:815. Cf. 3:771-76 for the Cumberland Confession.

8. George P. Hays, *Presbyterians, a Popular Narrative of Their Origin, Progress, and Achievements* (New York: J. A. Hill and Company, 1892), 151.

9. Ibid., 384.

10. *A Brief History of the Synod of Tennessee from 1817 to 1887* (Philadelphia: MacCalla & Company, 1890), 32-33, cited by Thompson, *Presbyterians*, 409.

11. Ibid., 412.

12. James Henry Thornwell, *Collected Writings* (Richmond: Presbyterian Committee of Publication, 1881), 4:210.

13. Cited from *Minutes of the General Assembly (O.S.) 1843*, 183.

14. See Thornwell, *Collected Writings*.

15. *Minutes of the General Assembly (O.S.) 1845*, 16-17.

16. *Minutes of the General Assembly (O.S.) 1861*, 16-17.

17. Ibid., 340.

18. Thomas Carey Johnson, *The Life and Letters of Benjamin Morgan Palmer* (Richmond, VA: n.p., 1906), 502.

19. *Minutes, PCUS, 1870*, 529; also in *Alexander's Digest, 1888*, 451, and in *Digest 1861-1965*, 342.

20. *Minutes PCCSA, 1861*, 17.

2

ROBERT LEWIS DABNEY

DOUGLAS FLOYD KELLY

Photo courtesy of Presbyterian Study Center.

Robert Lewis Dabney

ROBERT Lewis Dabney was perhaps the greatest, and certainly the most prolific, Southern Presbyterian theologian of nineteenth-century America. Reformed theologians of Europe such as Lecerf, Bavinck, and Barth spoke of Dabney with appreciation and respect. The great Charles Hodge of Princeton so highly regarded Dabney that he repeatedly urged him to join the Princeton faculty in 1860. In later years, A. A. Hodge and W. G. T. Shedd considered Dabney to be the greatest teacher of theology in the United States. B. B. Warfield said: ". . . Dr. Dabney was not only an influential statesman and a powerful ecclesiastical force, not only an acute philosophiser and a profound theologian, but also a devoted Christian—which is best of all."[1]

Yet for all his massive abilities, voluminous writings, and widespread personal prestige, Dabney lived to see his own theological and ecclesiastical influence drastically wane, so that near the end of his life he could sadly say: "I have no audience."[2] From his death in 1898 until the early 1960s, Dabney's work was largely eclipsed in his own denomination, not to mention the wider church. The reasons for his rise to prominence and then his rather drastic decline are found primarily in his theological stance and secondarily in the events and attitudes of his own eventful life and times.

Dabney's Life

While much of Dabney's *Systematic Theology*, for instance, is in the standard Reformed idiom and thus speaks for itself, it would be very difficult—if not impossible—to understand his social, economic, and political philosophy as well as many of his more directly religious essays unless we took into account the cultural and historical context of his life in the Old South. Unlike many theologians who pass their lives in sequestered libraries and classrooms, Dabney, like Abraham Kuyper of Holland, lived much of his life in public positions during tumultuous times.

His biographer, Thomas Cary Johnson, wrote:

> The lives even of most great preachers pass in such quiet that the historian finds little to dwell upon. What he says of one day's labor and achievements may be said of almost every other day. Such was not the life of Dr. Dabney. His life touched so many points in the common history of church and state and touched them in a way so unusual that it is impossible to give an adequate sketch in a few pages.[3]

Dabney was born March 5, 1820, on South Anna River in Louisa County, Virginia, the fourth of six children. His parents, Charles and Elizabeth Dabney, were typical Virginia country gentry. Charles was Colonel of the county militia, as well as a magistrate and member of the county court. He owned a tobacco and grain plantation, two mills, and several slaves, and was an elder in the Presbyterian Church. The older Dabneys had been brought up during times of revival in Virginia (the latter years of the "Second Great Awakening"), and maintained a strict but warmly evangelical household. In this Calvinist home not only were the Bible and Westminster Shorter Catechism taught, but the children "caught" the principles of conservative, decentralized republican forms of government from frequent conversations between their parents and visitors. The Virginia of Washington, Madison, Jefferson, Henry, and Marshall had never ceased to be politically minded and intensely committed to the liberties guaranteed (to the property-holding classes) by constitutional, representative civil government.

In the Dabney home there was a mingling of Calvinist simplicity and Puritan hard work with an element of aristocratic leisure based on the "peculiarly southern" institution of domestic slavery. Dabney grew up deeply loving the life and institutions of his native Virginia and of the larger antebellum South. It was to him the ideal blending of plainness and modesty with the richness of genuine Christian culture. Dabney once wrote an entire letter describing the surprised reaction of a "proud New Yorker" to the unexpected gentility and culture of Richmond society.[4]

Life became much harder for the Dabney family when the father, Charles, died in early middle age in 1833. Robert, then age 13, had to take on a good deal of responsibility for the management of the plantation and the well-being of his brothers and sisters. His letters show that strong cords of mutual affection bound this family together to the last.

In the midst of all his responsibilities, young Robert Dabney received a very competent education for his time and place:

> He received his preparatory training in country schools taught by his brother and other able men. The schedule of studies did not cover many lines, but very thorough work was done in Latin, Greek, Algebra, and Geometry. His zeal led him to ride once a week to get Dr. Thomas Wharey, his mother's pastor, to drill him in Mathematics.
>
> He spent a short time at Hampden-Sydney College; it covered three sessions, as the course then ran . . . (in 1836 and 1837). . . . He finished Mathematics, Physics, Latin and Greek. When he left the college the faculty sent his mother a report and assigned him the most distinguished rank in behavior, and the most distinguished rank in industry. He was the only one of his class so highly ranked.[5]

Toward the end of his time at Hampden-Sydney "the college was visited by a powerful and genuine awakening." Dabney was converted during this revival in September of 1837, and many years later commented that "The most important event of this period to me was my profession of faith in Christ."[6]

Dabney left Hampden-Sydney without completing his course in order to come home and help his mother improve the precarious financial position of their plantation. For about two years Robert, though a slaveholder, worked with his hands quarrying stone, rebuilt one of the family mills, managed the fields, and in addition opened and taught a neighborhood school—all of this at age 18!

Dabney's education was not finished, however,

> . . . because he found a way to enter the University of Virginia at Charlottesville. His uncle, Reuben Lewis, living near the University, had offered to give him board for himself and horse. The University offered fuller courses of study under more distinguished professors. . . . On July 5, 1842, he received his degree of Master of Arts. His study had made him a thinker.[7]

Robert returned to his mother's plantation for two more years of physical work, teaching of classes, and newspaper writing. He did so well as a writer that he was offered a job with one of the largest papers in the state—a forerunner of greater things to come. During this time he managed to save a few hundred dollars; this he was to spend on his subsequent education for the Presbyterian ministry.

> In November, 1844, he entered Union Seminary at Hampden-Sydney, Va. This institution was under a cloud of depression. There were only three professors: Dr. Samuel B. Wilson was Professor of Systematic and Polemic Theology, Dr. Samuel L. Graham of Eccle-

> siastical History, Dr. Francis R. Sampson of Oriental Literature. There were only eighteen students. Some from Virginia and North Carolina were at Columbia and Princeton. Mr. Dabney chose the smaller Seminary, for he believed in building up home institutions.[8]

By this time American Presbyterianism had divided into two major streams: New School and Old School. New School Presbyterianism, largely—though not entirely—in the North, was more open to the spirit of the age, and accommodated itself theologically to some aspects of Arminianism and other elements of post-Enlightenment thought. The Old School, which comprised a slight majority in the North and a vast majority in the South, cordially and strictly held to the robust Calvinism of the Westminster standards, and consciously saw itself as challenging the errors of the age. The Presbyterian Church in America had split over this very issue in 1837. Union Seminary, like its more illustrious northern sister, Princeton Seminary, was solidly in the Old School camp.

Perhaps the greatest single influence on young Dabney at Union was the fine scholar and pious saint, Dr. Francis R. Sampson. One of Dabney's first major writings was to be the biography of Sampson in 1854. "In mature old age Dr. Dabney wrote: 'If I ever had any intellectual growth and vigor, I owed it to three things—first, the Master of Arts' Course in the University of Virginia; second, to Dr. F. R. Sampson, and third, to my subsequent mastery of Turretin.' "[9]

In the summer of 1846 Dabney finished his studies at Union and was licensed by West Hanover Presbytery. His Latin thesis was "Quomodo Homo Justificatus Sit?" and his Greek exegesis on Hebrews 6:4-6. Although Dabney was a tall, large-framed man, his health at this stage was rather poor and his life was not expected to be a long one. Thus the Presbytery assigned him to three small, remote congregations as a home missionary in his native Louisa County. In spite of his poor health, his ministrations here were very faithful and warmly appreciated.

In 1847 Dabney was called to be pastor of the Tinkling Spring Church in Augusta County, near Staunton, Virginia. He had an effective ministry here among the (at times) headstrong Scotch-Irish for over six years. During this time of hard study, continual pastoral work, and diligent exegetical preaching attended by deep and agonizing prayer, many blessings entered into the life of pastor and congregation. Dabney was the architect for a new church building (which still stands); he met Miss Lavinia Morrison, daughter of a neighboring minister, whom he loved at first sight and soon married; and to crown it all a revival broke out in the church in 1850, during which over 30 persons were brought to Christ.

Dabney demonstrated his practical bent and many-sided abilities by building his own house out of stone that he himself had cut. "He was a good practical farmer, a good teacher, a good pastor, a capital member of a military staff. He was a skillful mechanic and furniture maker. . . . He bound books well, drew maps and plans for buildings."[10]

In 1853, at the age of 33, Dabney was called to the Chair of Ecclesiastical History and Polity at Union Seminary in Hampden-Sydney. For the next thirty years this was to be the scene of his major life's work as teacher, writer, churchman, statesman, soldier, and—above all—theologian.

> With characteristic energy he prepared a course of study that made young men master the facts and principles of history. He impressed the importance of acquiring good habits of study, as a preparation for life. He made such a reputation that in a few years he was invited to teach at Princeton, but he declined it.
>
> He spent his vacations in traveling through Virginia and North Carolina seeking students, funds and the support of presbyteries and congregations. By 1859 the number of students had increased to fifty-nine, new professors had been secured. . . . Never again was the Seminary considered as a liability, but a great asset.
>
> He was called to the presidency of Hampden-Sydney College in 1858, to the Fifth Avenue Church of New York in 1860, and also to Princeton in 1860, but he remained at Union.[11]

In 1859 Dabney was transferred to the Chair of Theology, which he undertook with enthusiasm, immense competence, and fresh vitality. Dabney believed that Systematic Theology must be based fairly and squarely upon an exegesis of the Scriptures. In an article in 1856, Dabney described the work of both professors and students at Union Seminary:

> . . . each professor shall be required to expound some portion of the original Scriptures. This is important to the teacher himself, that he may be brought into immediate contact with the Word of God. . . . Exegetical study is the great means for cultivating a right literary spirit in the theologian.[12]
>
> The student begins with the great fact that the Word of God (in the originals) is the grand repository of all the *data* of the science of divinity. . . . the Professor of Systematic and Pastoral Theology . . . teaches him, with the Bible still in his hand to methodize and understand the mutual relations of the Scripture facts and doctrines that they may assume in his mind the strength of *a system*.[13]

Dabney taught by means of dialogue. Two days before he lectured on a subject he wrote on the board a series of questions for his students. (Many of these questions are preserved at the beginning of each of the chapters in his *Systematic Theology*.) Along with the questions Dabney gave the students specific readings in various theologians—especially

Turretin in Latin and Dick in English. The class had to answer the questions in writing, which Dabney corrected; then he lectured on the subject.

During these years Dabney also served as copastor of the College Church, and was beginning to turn out a good deal of writing, especially in church periodicals. The pleasant though demanding routine of his scholarly life was soon to be interrupted by a momentous event that would change not only his own life, but that of the entire nation: the bitter and devastating War Between the States from 1861-1865.

The causes of this War are highly complex, but perhaps primarily revolved around the question of states' rights versus centralized national authority. Many in the South believed that the northern states were taking unfair advantage of the Union to advance their own economic interests (through tariffs, for instance), and that the various states had the constitutional right to withdraw from the Union; whereas many in the North felt that the states had no such rights, and that the power of the central government should be used to abolish southern slavery.

At first, Dabney—like most Virginians (and unlike most South Carolinians)—was a moderate on the question of both slavery and withdrawal.[14] Just before the outbreak of hostilities he joined with other evangelical ministers of both North and South in pleading with Christians in all parts of America to pray and do all they could to avoid fratricidal conflict.[15] In his earlier years he certainly favored the gradual emancipation of all slaves.[16] When the War did break out, however, Dabney committed himself wholeheartedly to the southern cause. His thinking became increasingly partisan and colored by all the emotion and vehemence of the "underdog" in this painful and deathly struggle. For the rest of his life he would believe that the southern cause was totally righteous and that "Yankeedom" was totally wicked.

Dabney firmly believed that the War was caused by the French Revolution "Jacobin" principles of New England Unitarian abolitionists and their liberal congressional "hacks," who wished to turn the original constitutional republic with its emphasis on state and local power into a secularized, centralized democratic power.[17] While a recent work by historian Otto Scott[18] indicates that there was at least an element of truth in this assessment, nonetheless Dabney's attitude was a gross oversimplification and in a sense ignored—or treated with contempt—the vital question of how the rest of the world felt about the morality of slavery.[19]

Not only was Dabney a literary apologist for the South and preacher to the troops, but for a while he served on the front lines as Chief of Staff to the famous Confederate general and pious Presbyterian deacon, Thomas J. "Stonewall" Jackson. Jackson said that Dabney was the most efficient officer he ever had.[20] Before the War ended, Dabney wrote a large and popular biography of Jackson. Not long after, he wrote *A De-*

fense of Virginia and Through Her of the South, which showed that slavery was not explicitly condemned by the Scriptures as sinful, and argued that it had been the most beneficial economic and moral system for all concerned in the South.

From a strictly exegetical viewpoint, Dabney was right that the Scriptures never specifically condemned slavery, and yet in retrospect it seems strange and sad that he and the other southern defenders of slavery totally failed to come to terms with the implications of the biblical Jubilee—that a slave who became a brother in the faith must be given his freedom after seven years since he is now in the covenant[21]—and with the equally important fact that Christianity established new moral and social conditions that would render personal bondage unacceptable. Unlike Professor Frank Bell Lewis, who felt that Dabney's major failure at this point was his identification with the conservative Bibliocentrism of nineteenth-century Virginia rather than with the more liberal Jeffersonian tradition of eighteenth-century Virginia, we would suggest that Dabney was not overly biblical on this subject; on the contrary, he did not go as far as his Bible should have taken him.[22] Like all other fallen men, including theologians, he had blind spots where his devotion to the culture made it difficult for him to interpret the will of God.

After the bitter defeat of the South in 1865 and then the agony and humiliation of impoverishing Reconstruction, much of Dabney's life seemed to be lived under deepening shadows. He seriously considered emigrating from the United States, but decided to stay. As his biographer says, for the rest of his life "he was at war with much in his age."[23]

The eighteenth-century secularist Enlightenment and its nineteenth-century European developments were bringing vast changes in the Western world, and it seems clear that the War between the States hastened the breakdown of the relative isolation and conservative Christian consensus of the American South. "French" political radicalism, "German" Higher Criticism of the Scriptures, and "British" evolutionism were all influencing the intellectual classes of America, while a broad, basically Arminian type of evangelicalism with new methodologies (developed by evangelists Finney and Moody) was deeply influencing the popular classes. In the philosophical world, the very possibility of objective knowledge of reality—and specifically of any true knowledge of a personal God—was being radically questioned and excluded from consideration. Dabney waged vigorous and vehement war against all of these powerful, secularizing trends of the century.

Almost never an obscurantist, Dabney carefully read the works of the enemies of biblical Calvinism, and traced their errors down to their poisonous roots. He had a wide interest and a mind that could successfully grapple with complex issues in philosophy, logic, sociology, and economics. He brought vigorous, and at times caustic and scathing criticism to bear on humanistic and Arminian trends. He offered uncompromising, and sometimes painful, solutions from the Word of God to a remarkably broad variety of questions.

While his analysis and solutions were generally well grounded biblically, and not infrequently manifested a radically brilliant insight, nevertheless his stringent tone, inflexibility, and on occasion lack of proper tact alienated many who otherwise might have fought on his side. On the other hand, a careful reading of his life and times will indicate that the basic reason for his increasing lack of popularity (even among his own Southern Presbyterians) was not his all too real failures of tone and tact, but his uncompromising, public insistence on total loyalty to the traditional biblical Calvinism that was becoming an embarrassment to the post-Enlightenment, broadening Evangelical mainstream that was inundating all of America's churches, the Reformed included.

Although he had had the honor of serving the (Southern) Presbyterian Church in the United States as Moderator in 1870, and had continued to publish widely read articles and significant books, still he was swimming against the mainstream as he opposed any sort of union with the Northern Presbyterian Church; as he opposed public education (as inherently secularist); as he opposed Moody/Sankey type "revivals"; and as he continued to oppose social and business accommodation of Southerners with the increasingly dominant "Yankee" capitalistic economy and culture.[24] By 1883 Dabney keenly felt "his loss of influence at the Seminary."[25] According to Frank B. Lewis, the Seminary authorities "had refused to accept his proposals for the future of that institution"; Dabney "felt himself isolated from the main currents of the life of the Southern Church," and "his long list of controversies had won him the reputation of being cantankerous."[26] In addition to this, his health was bad and his doctors advised a drier climate.

Thus (we can imagine with much sadness and frustration) he accepted a call to teach at the University of Texas in Austin, in the Chair of Moral and Mental Philosophy. While there in the final stage of his ever active life, he organized the Theological Seminary of Austin and wrote very widely in the fields of sociology, politics, philosophy, and economics.[27] In 1889 he became completely blind, but was able to continue teaching, preaching, and writing. As Dabney remained thoroughly conservative and Calvinist, however, the University of Texas was moving in a more liberal direction.[28] Because of this, in what was undoubtedly a parable of his life, Dabney was asked to resign in 1894. He continued to lecture and write, and two significant books came from his pen within a year of his death in 1898: *The Atonement* and *The Practical Philosophy*.

Dabney as a Theologian and Philosopher

Dabney's theological approach and methodology is remarkably similar to that of the Westminster standards: it is biblical (and to a degree exegetical), it is moderate and nonspeculative, and it faces the hardest questions while attempting to avoid harshness. If Dabney made extreme statements (and he did), these were made in the realm of politics and social philosophy, but almost never in theology. He wrote his theology the way standard church confessions are written—with the larger Reformed and Christian community in mind. Dabney certainly followed the advice of the Scottish Commissioner Henderson to the Westminster Assembly of the 1640s: "Let us avoid all scholastical disputes and unnecessary distinctions."

Dabney nobly exemplifies in his own theology what he says about the enduring quality of the Westminster standards:

> . . . The second marked trait of the Confession (is) its doctrinal moderation. . . . The Assembly . . . was too wise to attempt the conciliating of opposites by the surrendering of any essential member of the system of revealed truth. They present us the Pauline, Augustinian or Calvinist creed in its integrity. But on the other hand, they avoid every excess and every extreme statement. They refrained with a wise moderation from committing the Church of God on either side of those "*isms*" which agitated and perplexed the professors of the Reformed Theology.

Then Dabney illustrates the moderation of the Westminster Confession on the disputed questions of the Being and providence of God, supra- and infralapsarianism, mediate and immediate imputation, and general eschatology, which avoids commitment to either post- or premillennial theories.[29]

Dabney's lifelong insistence on balance, nonspeculation, and moderation in theological statement seems to come in part from his old Seminary predecessor, Baxter, in part from the Scottish theologian whose work he continually used, John Dick, and also from the Westminster standards themselves. Based on an analysis of his *Systematic Theology*, Lewis shows that of the more than 150 authors referred to by Dabney, those most frequently appealed to were—in this order—Turretin, Dick, Hill, Hodge, Knapp, Watson, Ridgeley, Calvin, Thornwell, and Witsius.[30] We note an absence of reference to his contemporary Dutch theologians, and very little direct interaction with any of the Fathers of the Greek or Latin Church (and in this, he and most other nineteenth-century American Reformed theologians were unlike Calvin). He does, however, make use of both Anselm and Thomas Aquinas in the original. Certainly Dabney did not mind differing from Calvin, Edwards, Dick, Hodge, and other respected Reformed scholars, although he did not seem to delight in differing, for instance, from Hodge in the way Thornwell appeared at times to do.

Another constituent element of Dabney's theological method was his adherence to the Scottish Common Sense Philosophy of Realism. He comments on this commitment extensively in his *Sensualistic Philosophy of the Nineteenth Century*, where he opposes the skeptical conclusions of the various forms of empirical and associational psychology and philosophy by means of the assumption of the original powers of the mind to form valid judgments that penetrate reality on the basis of data presented to the mind through the senses. Dabney saw the crux of the question as whether the mind can know objective truth:

> It is related that when the plan of Locke's Essay was first reported to his great contemporary, Leibniz, before the book had yet appeared in Germany, and the narrator stated that all was founded on a literal acceptance of the old scholastic law, *Nihil in intellectu quod non prius in sensu*, the great German replied, *Etiam, nisi intellectus ipse*. These words contain the key to the whole discussion. . . . In attempting to enumerate the affections of the mind, it overlooked the mind itself. . . .
>
> The *Ego* is a real existence. If our cognitions have any regular method, then it must be by virtue of some primary principles of cognition which are subjective to the mind. While we claim no "innate ideas", yet it is evident that the intelligence has some innate norms, which determine the nature of its processes, whenever the objective world presents the occasion of them. To deny this, we must not only believe the absurdity of regular series of effects without any regulative cause in their subject; but we must also deny totally the spontaneity of the mind.[31]

Thus, following Reid, Dabney presupposed the reality and validity of the mind, and the reality of cause and effect. Rather like Cornelius Van Til (who was born the decade Dabney died), Dabney showed that even to argue against these premises, one had to use them, and thus: "None but theists can consistently use induction."[32] Also like the later theologian Van Til, Dabney demonstrated that nontheists, too, reasoned on the basis of unproven, faith assumptions: "He who declares that science cannot have any *a priori* truths, virtually adopts as his *a priori* truth the ground maxim of that psychology. . . ."[33]

> These recent unbelievers admit the established facts; but, having approached them with the foregone conclusion that there can be no supernatural cause, they are reduced, for a pretended explanation, to a set of unproved hypotheses and fantastic guesses, which they offer us for verities, in most ludicrous contradiction to the very spirit of their "positive philosophy."[34]

Again he is like Van Til and Kuyper in showing the inevitable bias of the human mind against God's truth because of its commitment to a self-serving conceptual framework:

> . . . all who reason can see that no moral conclusion can be a pure intellection, but that some voluntary element must enter for good or for evil into the sources of every such judgment. No man on earth reasons towards objects which he either likes or dislikes strongly, with the same complete intellectual impartiality with which he reasons about pure mathematics. . . . All people, while agreeing perfectly upon the truths of mathematics and numbers, differ more or less upon questions of property rights, law-suits, character, politics, medicine, and religion. It is because all these objects of thought involve elements which appeal to the feelings and the will.[35]

If Dabney had affinities with the presuppositional school of Kuyper and Van Til on the analysis of human reasoning, his views of natural theology and apologetics were certainly unlike theirs, and followed in the general line of Aquinas, Butler, Alexander, Chalmers, and Hodge. He followed the traditional Catholic and Reformed approach of first studying natural, and then revealed theology. It is perhaps here that his reliance upon Scottish Realism most shows through, when for example he establishes the traditional proofs for God's existence on the basis of cause and effect in the line of Thomas Reid against the arguments of Hume. Interestingly, Dabney, like Aquinas, did not favor the ontological argument for God's existence.

In his natural theology Dabney has very little, if anything, original or fresh to say, and like most natural theologians quietly imports a good deal of content from Scripture as to the Being and ways of God (which would be exceedingly difficult to see in nature unless one already knew the Scriptures). There are two areas, however, which stand on the border of natural and revealed theology, where he had some bright insights (which he did not develop systematically). These areas would later be developed in the twentieth century by thinkers such as Van Til and Francis Schaeffer on the one hand and Thomas F. Torrance on the other.[36]

As though he were anticipating Van Til, Schaeffer, and others, Dabney deals in a helpful way with the question of how a finite human mind can think and know the Infinite. This question was occasioned by Dabney's reaction to the Scottish philosopher Sir William Hamilton, who on this matter was influenced more by Kant than by Reid, and held that the limited mind cannot think "unconditioned" or infinite Being.[37] Dabney makes it clear that we can know truly that which is infinite without knowing completely or exhaustively.

> The finite mind would need to become infinite, in order to contain a complete and exhaustive conception of any infinite being. But we

> do not claim such a conception. The finite mind may remain finite, and yet contain an incomplete, yet valid, apprehension of infinite being.[38]

The use of the word "apprehension" shows the deep insight of Dabney into the roots of this question (as opposed to the word "comprehension"). In his *Systematic Theology* Dabney explores in greater detail the important epistemological difference between apprehension (which finite minds can do of the infinite) and comprehension (which they cannot).[39] But even if the human mind only claims to apprehend God (rather than comprehend him), on what basis can one claim that even *that* is possible (as someone like Mansel, the follower of Hamilton and Kant, would have argued)?

Dabney clearly sees that the answer lies in the direction of man's creation in the image of God. God is infinite and personal, and man is finite but, because created in God's image, also personal. Thus, in spite of the difference between infinity and finitude, the personal can know the personal.[40] This would be developed more clearly in the next century by scholars such as Van Til and Schaeffer, but this insight was already an important element in the epistemology of Dabney.

Dabney also manifested penetrating insight into a second boundary area between natural and revealed theology, into what Thomas F. Torrance has called the necessary and irreducible "triadic structure of revelation" (i.e., God, man, *and* nature).[41] That is, Dabney clearly pointed out that any objectively valid revelation from God to man always involves the structures of created nature. Thus nature, far from being an embarrassment and hindrance to revelation, is its medium. Dabney deals with this important epistemological matter when he comments on the widespread biblical phenomenon of anthropomorphism, which was such an offense to the nineteenth-century idealism that depreciated nature as well as history ("the eternal truths of reason can never be expressed in the accidental facts of history"). The cutting off of Jesus and the church from their roots in Judaism, the desupernaturalizing of Christ and the Scriptures, and then the ultimate loss of "the historical Jesus" and consequent denial of the Incarnation were all part and parcel of the idealistic assumption that eternal reality and truth cannot be validly expressed and apprehended in the structures of nature and history.

In the course of his argumentation against Hume, Mill, and Spencer (on their denial of causation as a theistic proof), Dabney goes to the root of the matter of anthropomorphism and the very possibility of divine revelation in the created order:

> . . . if God has made the human mind "after His image, in His likeness," this would effectually guarantee all our legitimately ra-

> tional processes of thought against vice from *anthropomorphism*. For, in thinking according to the natural laws of our minds, we would be thinking precisely as God bids us think. . . . The unreasonableness of the demand, that we shall reject any conception of the divine working, though reached by normal (human) inference, merely because it may be anthropomorphic, appears thus. It would equally forbid us to think or learn at all, either concerning God, or any other Being or concept different from man: for, if we are not allowed to think in the forms of thought natural and normal for us, we are forbidden to think at all. All man's cognition must be anthropomorphic, or nothing.[42]

He makes the same point, in a more directly theological way, in his *Systematic Theology:*

> But when the inspired witness, the Bible, comes to us, with attestation, (by miracles, prophecies, &c.,) exactly suited to the forms of the human understanding, and assures us that our spirits are made in the likeness of God's, all fear of our theology, as made invalid by anthropomorphism, is removed. And especially when we are shown the Messiah, as the image of the invisible God, and hear Him reason, we have a complete verification.[43]

Dabney does not deal with some of the related philosophical problems involved in this concept of the essential triadic structure of revelation. Moreover, he does not even begin to develop in a systematic manner the epistemological and theological ramifications of it as T. F. Torrance does a century later, but his profound theological discernment certainly pointed him in the right direction.

In his voluminous work in the area of revealed theology, Dabney's approach may be consistently characterized as thoroughly conservative and displaying contempt for all innovation and speculation. Dabney adhered so closely in both letter and spirit to the Westminster standards that in a speech before the Southern Presbyterian General Assembly the last year of his life, he could seriously make this very strong assertion: ". . . the Confession will need no amendment until the Bible needs to be amended."[44] On the other hand, Dabney saw himself as above all a biblical and exegetical theologian. While he was not like a Geerhardus Vos, for example, who took into profound consideration the reality of progressive, historical development of revelation within the Scriptures themselves, he was in some respects a forerunner of great exegetical theologians such as B. B. Warfield and John Murray, who were prepared to question received Reformed terminology and concepts in light of careful word study and contextual opening of a passage. That is, on many occasions (though far from always) Dabney can be looked on as something of a bridge between the earlier traditional prooftexting of a Turretin and the later contextual, exegetical research of Warfield and Vos.[45] Many examples of the sort of faithful grappling with a text that yields sound exegetical theology can be pointed out in Dabney.[46] A model of his exegetical openness is his treatment of John 3:16, in which he differs with the traditional interpretation of such great Reformed theologians as John Owen in refusing to restrict the meaning of "world" to "all the elect."[47] Because of his careful exegetical study of some aspects of Bible covenants, Dabney in a certain sense seems to have anticipated the work of John Murray and others in stressing the very close relationship between the Mosaic and Abrahamic Covenants.[48] Granted Dabney's own consistent exegetical emphasis in theology, it is not surprising that he preferred, as Frank B. Lewis has pointed out, scriptural rather than speculative theologians.[49]

Closely related to Dabney's submission to the plain text of Scripture and his commitment to the sober and moderate Calvinism of the Westminster standards is his continual disavowal of all types of theological speculation—Reformed speculation included! Many are the places where Dabney says (over against the distinctions between infra- and supralapsarianism, mediate and immediate imputation, creationism and traducianism, etc.), ". . . this is a question which never ought to have been raised."[50] Here he follows the spirit of Calvin rather than of Beza and Gomarus.

In accordance with his moderate, non–"hyper"-Calvinism, and unlike the stringent spirit of some of his political and social statements, Dabney labors very hard to avoid all harshness as he faces the hard questions of theology. For instance, he definitely wishes to leave the door open to the possibility of the universal salvation of all who die in infancy.[51] He does not like the thought involved in the term "Limited" Atonement, and while he clearly affirms the "particular redemption" of the elect, still he prefers (against Dr. William Cunningham of Scotland) to hold to a certain "general design" in the atonement, a "sincere offer of mercy," and "a sense in which Christ 'died for' all those ends, and for the persons affected by them."[52]

Following John Dick of Scotland, Dabney attempts to describe the decree of reprobation in the mildest terms possible, omitting condemnation from the decree.[53] He criticizes his great contemporary, Charles Hodge of Princeton, for the undue harshness implied in his scheme of immediate imputation of the sin of Adam to his offspring.[54] Dabney dislikes any viewpoint of election that underrates or turns into a fiction the genuine pity and mercy of God for lost sinners.[55] Likewise he repudiates all "hyper-" systems that refrain from urging lost sinners to seek the face of God and pray.[56]

Apparently with no trepidation, Dabney enters the lists of the traditional argument (which ran through such varied schools as Plato, the New England Puritans, A. E. Taylor, and Van Til) over whether something is morally right because God commands it, or does he command it because it is right? Unlike most of the Puritans, and more in the line of Plato, Dabney thinks it sounds too harshly arbitrary to say that right is right because God wills it.[57] Of course he carefully states that he does not mean that there is a standard outside or above God. Still, Dabney seems to be lacking his usual penetration of the issues here, and out of fear of harsh overtones does not seem able to appreciate the important point being raised by the Puritans. Certainly his disagreement with the Puritans is merely terminological and not substantial, but he has not grasped, or simply dissents from, the propriety of their terminological concern.

As we would expect in a noninnovator, most of Dabney's work in the various topics of revealed theology is not notably different from the position of his scholastic Calvinist predecessors and his great conservative Reformed contemporaries. Some parts of his thought, nevertheless, do deserve comment. There are at least two areas of the theological curriculum where Dabney appears to have made some real contributions, especially in the sense of stating in a fresh, clear, and generally attractive way complex and difficult truths, and there is a third area where, in terms of the contribution of Calvin himself, Dabney's thought seems to miss the mark.

The late Professor John Murray of Westminster reportedly considered his own major contribution to Reformed theology to have been in the area of anthropology: especially the question of the Adamic Administration.[58] A careful reading of Dabney's *Systematic Theology*, *Sensualistic Philosophy of the Nineteenth Century*, and *Practical Philosophy* would seem to indicate that Dabney's fullest contribution to the development of the traditional Reformed theological curriculum also lies in the area of anthropology: particularly in his description of the *habitus* of the personality and also in his minute work on the place of the feelings in the human makeup.

Dabney's work on the *habitus* is usually in the context of such questions as free will, natural inability and moral responsibility, divine providence and human spontaneity, the influence of regeneration on the intellect and will, and the general causative effects of the character on human thought and action. In the course of these discussions, Dabney at times finds himself disagreeing with and correcting fellow Reformed scholars such as Hodge, Thornwell, and Dick.

By *habitus* Dabney essentially meant the basic dispositional and motivational complex at the roots of the human personality that determines what one's character is and thus what one's choices and actions are.[59] Dabney felt that he was being more consistently clear than Dick, Thornwell, or Hodge in showing that the entire soul is a unity (or "monad") both in its unregenerate and regenerate states,[60] and that if this unity is not kept in the forefront of a Christian anthropology, then confusion will result in several areas. Therefore, Dabney clarifies or corrects confused thinking in some areas of the theology of Dick (on the inability of the natural man to understand Scripture), of Thornwell (on the will's natural inability and the righteousness of God), of Hodge (on the illumination of the mind and depravity of the whole soul), and of the controversial southern minister and writer Bledsoe in dialogue with Jonathan Edwards (on the freedom and spontaneity of the will).[61] Dabney's writings on the effects of regeneration on the whole character (based on the change of dispositional *habitus*) are marked by a lucidity and pungency in the line of the old Scottish divine, Thomas Boston.[62]

Given Dabney's interest in and study of human psychology (especially in his *Practical Philosophy* and *Sensualistic Philosophy*), it comes as no surprise that he has much clarity and several insights to contribute to Reformed theological anthropology in the area of the feelings. Unlike those forms of rationalistic theology (whether of the liberal or fundamentalist variety) that tend to treat the human mind as though it were in neutral abstraction from the complex motivations and feelings of the moral character, Dabney perceives the immense moral, epistemological, and theological importance and influence of man's subjective emotions. Dabney knew that feelings were important and required careful analysis and consideration as a part of the theological curriculum because:

> Essentially, feelings are man's motive power. Intellect is the cold and latent magnetism which directs the ship's compass. . . . Feeling is that elastic energy which throbs within the machinery, and gives propulsion to its wheels. . . . The vigor of the functions of cognition itself depends, in every man, more on the force of the incentive energizing the faculty, than on the native strength or clearness of the intellect. . . . It is chiefly the feelings which make the man.[63]

Dabney carefully examines and categorizes the feelings and judges them to be expressions of man's basic character disposition (or *habitus*).[64] These basic motivational expressions are then related to man's moral obligation or conscience. The relationships and inner workings of basic character, feelings, and conscience are made central to Dabney's system of ethics, and his insights into these interconnections seem often to enable him to "get inside" the motivations, problems, and responsibilities of human beings individually and socially.[65]

Dabney's close study of the feelings, for instance, enables him to give a penetrating analysis of "spurious religious feelings" in which he sheds burning light on carnal, selfish feelings in religion.[66] Dabney's work at this point should be studied by all who have to deal with the "prosperity teaching" of some segments of the "Electronic Church" in America. He offers interesting thoughts on how immersion in emotional novels (today we might substitute "soap operas") can degenerate genuine sentiment into cheap sentimentality, which weakens the vigor of the moral resolve when one goes back into the real world.[67]

In addition to his contribution in the realm of Reformed anthropology, Dabney also clarifies, and in that sense develops, another topic of classical theology: providence. His basic area of concern is the *concursus* between God's sovereign, primary control of all things, and the reality and validity of human and natural secondary causation. In his *Systematic Theology* he deals with the question "How God's effective providence can intervene consistently with the uniformity of natural laws"[68] in a way that he believes is clearer than the expositions of Dick, Hodge, and McCosh.[69] He also corrects what he feels are defects in the doctrine of the physical *concursus* of God in evil as well as in good acts and physical causes, which was held by his great mentor Turretin of seventeenth-century Geneva, and by the Dutch Calvinist Witsius (who followed a false lead from Aquinas at this point).[70]

As we see from his *Sensualistic Philosophy*, Dabney wishes to avoid a hypersupernaturalism that short-circuits moral effort and responsibility, while at the same time strongly affirming the traditional Calvinist doctrine of God's total sovereign control.[71] Dabney prefers not to speak of providence as "the supernatural violating of natural laws," but rather as God's perpetual superintendence of the "regular" law of nature.[72]

A third area of Dabney's work in the traditional theological curriculum deserves comment: his view of the sacraments. Here, in terms of Calvin's sacramental understanding, Dabney seems to take a step backward, giving future generations of Southern Presbyterians a generally weak or low view of the sacraments. Dabney finds Calvin's profound teaching on the powerful and gracious reality of the Holy Spirit's work in effectuating a sacramental union between the physical elements in the sacrament and the blessings of union with Christ's glorified human nature to be ". . . not only incomprehensible, but impossible."[73] Here, perhaps, his commitment to the categories of Scottish Common Sense Realism has restricted the usual depth and richness of his theological discernment. In his own day, a contemporary theologian from South Carolina, John B. Adger, answered this critique of Calvin's view of the sacraments, but still Dabney's viewpoint has predominated in the church.[74]

Dabney as Prophet and Social Critic

Dabney manifests a wider and deeper cultural, social, and political interest than any other theologian of nineteenth-century America. He was in a sense ahead of his time in spanning the fields of both sociology and religion. His penetrating theological critique of culture is at times like that of E. Rosenstock-Huessy and R. J. Rushdoony. While Thornwell and Shedd were more eloquent than Dabney, Hodge more influential, and B. M. Palmer a greater preacher, Dabney excels them all as a prophet. In a very limited yet real sense, Dabney was like Ezekiel and Jeremiah in that the development of his prophetic gift was very costly to himself: he passed through the fires of experiencing the bitter defeat of his homeland and the resultant breakup of the southern culture that was the pride and joy of his heart. This was both his strength and his weakness: the defeat of the South served to give him uncanny insight into the future problems of American culture, and at the same time tended so to wrench his emotions that his thought became prejudiced and his moral vision blinded in some very important areas of human life and endeavor.

Dabney's open hatred of the post-Civil War industrialization of American society made him an outsider to the developing cultural consensus, and strengthened the vision of his ever keen moral eye to penetrate the weaknesses of America's increasingly secularist materialism and industrialism. Dabney utilizes a strong, largely correct, and far from comforting critique of the evils of debt capitalism,[75] of the immoral use of the civil government by the industrial plutocracy to enforce monopolies that crushed smaller competitors,[76] of the dishonesty of monetary inflation,[77] of the treatment of man as a machine,[78] and of the certainty of the eventual de-Christianization and secularization of public school education.[79] Most sobering of all, he foresaw the coming, twentieth-century struggle in America for religious and civil liberties between a powerful centralized state with totalitarian temptations and a broad and shallow church that had forgotten the theological and constitutional basis of liberty.[80]

Dabney also had valid insights into the general weakening of Reformed theology and practice in the Calvinist churches of late nineteenth-century America. He foresaw impending problems with the weakening of Christian intellectual resistance to evolutionary speculation[81] and to higher criticism of the Scriptures,[82] the decline toward liberalism in the theological seminaries,[83] the decline of serious church discipline,[84] the growth of human inventions and the loss of real unction in worship,[85] and the bitter harvest to be reaped from humanly induced methods of more rapid and successful evangelism,[86] and he even discussed the development of the false split between Christ as Savior and Christ as Lord.[87] Dabney apparently offended many as he deplored the growing tendency of Christians to indulge themselves in luxury and to be forgetful of the poor.[88]

Much less happy in biblical insight was the deeply jaundiced viewpoint that Dabney turned upon the situation of the black people. In addition to supporting slavery before the War, he vehemently protested the ecclesiastical equality of black people as potential officers in white churches and presbyteries after the War.[89] He opposed tax-paid education for blacks in Virginia (but he opposed it for poor whites as well).[90] He held that the blacks were culturally inferior[91] (he seems to leave the question of whether they were personally inferior an open one), and hence he theorized that it would take untold generations before blacks could be raised to cultural equality with whites. This sort of attitude of course helped drive the black freedmen from white churches to the detriment of the unity of the body of Christ and healing of the nation.

In retrospect, it seems sadly shortsighted that Dabney could offer the people of the Reconstruction South such a clear solution from degeneracy in times of oppression, and yet fail to see that the very same solution should hold true of the blacks, who were also created in the image of God. In "The Duty of the Hour" Dabney advises:

> The correlated duty is that of anxiously preserving our integrity and self-respect. . . . The victims of unrighteous oppression, are usually degraded by their unavenged wrongs. . . . The man who has ceased to feel moral indignation for wrong has ceased to feel the claims of virtue. Nor is there a valid reason for your insensibility to evil, in the fact that you yourself are the object of it.[92]

Undoubtedly Dabney's greatest blind spot in this whole matter was, as Terry Johnson has pointed out, his underestimation of the power of the gospel in the life and culture of blacks (which can make saints, leaders, and heroes of them as well as of any other people).[93]

Dabney's prophecy, then, was both remarkably right and grievously wrong. As his close friend and biographer, T. C. Johnson, has pointed out, Dabney was often too pessimistic about the future of the church.[94] And as Charles R. Wilson has noted, Dabney failed to see that "a separate southern religion [would] survive in the postwar South, as a foundation for a distinctive southern culture."[95]

We whose unperceived blind spots will be deplored by future Christian generations will not speak too harshly of Dabney, who was marked by the fallenness of his own time and culture, as we are by ours. The way forward is to see beyond him by standing on his shoulders—and on those of all the saints and doctors of the church in all ages.

It is interesting to note that Dabney, who said "I have no audience" and described himself as "the Cassandra of Yankeedom,"[96] now, in the 1980s, has a larger audience than any time during his life. Indeed, since the mid-1960s nearly all of his works have been reprinted (in some cases, several times) on both sides of the Atlantic. Perhaps T. C. Johnson was right when he wrote some eighty years ago:

Dr. Dabney was a great man. We cannot tell just how great yet. One cannot see how great Mt. Blanc is while standing at its foot. One hundred years from now men will be able to see him better.[97]

Notes: Robert Lewis Dabney

1. B. B. Warfield in *The Princeton Theological Review* (1905).

2. R. L. Dabney, *Discussions: Evangelical and Theological*, 2 vols. (London: The Banner of Truth Trust, 1962), 2:558.

3. Thomas Cary Johnson, *In Memoriam: R. L. Dabney* (Knoxville: University of Tennessee Press, 1898), 7.

4. Thomas Cary Johnson, *The Life and Letters of Robert Lewis Dabney* (Edinburgh: The Banner of Truth Trust, 1977 [1903]), 192.

5. C. T. Thompson, "Robert Lewis Dabney—The Conservative," *The Union Seminary Review* 35 (January 1924), 155-56.

6. Johnson, *Life and Letters*, 42-43.

7. Thompson, "R. L. Dabney," 156.

8. Ibid., 157.

9. Ibid.

10. Johnson, *Life and Letters*, 551.

11. Thompson, "R. L. Dabney," 159-60.

12. Johnson, *Life and Letters*, 153.

13. Ibid., 151-52.

14. Ibid., 210-34.

15. See "Christians, Pray for Your Country," in R. L. Dabney, *Discussions*, 2:393-400.

16. James H. Smylie, "The Burden of Southern Church Historians: World Mission, Regional Captivity, Reconciliation," *Journal of Presbyterian History* 46 (December 1968), 295.

17. Dabney regularly criticizes "Jacobinism," e.g., in *Discussions by Robert L. Dabney*, 4 vols. (Harrisonburg: Sprinkle Publications, 1979-1980), 4:542; 3:498ff.; *A Defence of Virginia and through Her the South* (Harrisonburg: Sprinkle Publications, 1977), 254; *Life and Campaigns of Lieut.-Gen. Thomas J. Jackson* (Harrisonburg: Sprinkle Publications, 1976), 162-69, 159-61; *The Sensualistic Philosophy of the Nineteenth Century* (Anson D. F. Randolph, 1887), 58.

18. Otto J. Scott, *The Secret Six: John Brown and the Abolitionist Movement* (New York: Times Books, 1979). Of course, some in the North saw the War as a southern, slaveholders' conspiracy; see William A. Clebsch, *Christian Interpretations of the Civil War* (Philadelphia: Fortress Press, 1969), 2, 6.

19. This is not to imply that Dabney does not deal openly and boldly with slavery, for he does in *Defence of Virginia* and elsewhere, but rather that he could not take seriously the moral challenge raised by nearly all other Christians throughout the Western world. Instead, he tended to discount the challenge as motivated by "Jacobinism" (or as we would say, "radical secular humanism").

20. Johnson, *Life and Letters*, 272.

21. Lev. 25:39-55. See also Exod. 21:2.

22. Frank Bell Lewis, *Robert Lewis Dabney: Southern Presbyterian Apologist* (Ph.D. diss., Duke University, 1946), 213-14.

23. Johnson, *Life and Letters*, 568.

24. See "The New South," in Dabney, *Discussions*, 4:1-24.

25. Smylie, "The Burden of Southern Church Historians," 292.

26. Lewis, *Robert Lewis Dabney*, 30.

27. See Dabney, *Discussions*, Vols. 3 and 4, and *Practical Philosophy*.

28. David H. Overy, *Robert Lewis Dabney: Apostle of the Old South* (Ph.D. diss., University of Wisconsin, 1967), 292-98.

29. Dabney, "The Doctrinal Contents of the Confession of Faith," in *Memorial Volume of the Westminster Assembly, 1647-1897* (Richmond, VA: The Presbyterian Committee of Publication, 1897), 95.

30. Lewis, *Robert Lewis Dabney*, 161.

31. Dabney, *Sensualistic Philosophy*, 248-49.

32. Ibid., 412.

33. Ibid., 97; see also p. 54 on J. S. Mill's circular reasoning.

34. Ibid., 100.

35. Dabney, *Discussions*, 4:512-13.

36. There is no line of direct thought from Dabney to these scholars. Their insights were not developed in dialogue with his writings.

37. See Dabney, *Sensualistic Philosophy*, ch. 10, esp. 216-17.

38. Ibid., 223.

39. Dabney, *Systematic Theology*, 149, also 138-39. Saint Hilary works with this distinction as early as the fourth century in the first two books of his *De Trinitate*, but it is highly unlikely that Dabney had read this. Hilary of course influenced Calvin, whom Dabney had read.

40. Dabney, *Sensualistic Philosophy*, 138-39, 230-31, 237-38, etc.

41. See, e.g., Thomas F. Torrance, *Reality and Evangelical Theology* (Philadelphia: The Westminster Press, 1982) and *God and Rationality* (London: Oxford University Press, 1971), ch. 4.

42. Dabney, *Sensualistic Philosophy*, 405-06. Again, early fathers such as Novatian of Rome in the third century had dealt very clearly with anthropomorphisms in terms of God's accommodation to man's littleness, and this had influenced Calvin, whom Dabney knew, if not Novatian.

43. Dabney, *Systematic Theology*, 295; see also his *Discussions*, 1:297.

44. Dabney, "Doctrinal Contents of the Confession of Faith," 94.

45. Probably Joseph Addison Alexander of Princeton, had he lived longer, would have been even more of a bridge in this direction than Dabney; but of course Alexander was not primarily a systematic theologian.

46. See, e.g., Dabney, *Discussions*, 1:238 (on repentance); ibid., 262-63 (on Rom. 5); ibid., 271 (on "sinned in Adam"); ibid., 312 (on John 3:16); ibid., 555ff. (an exposition of I Cor. 3:10-15); *Systematic Theology*, 34 (original sin); ibid., 35 (imputation of Adam's guilt); ibid., 207-08 (on the eternal generation of the Son); ibid., 386 (on Col. 2:16-17); ibid., 573-77 (on the "understanding" and the "heart"); ibid., 619ff. (good exegetical work on justification).

47. Dabney, *Systematic Theology*, 527-28, 535; *Discussions*, 1:311-13.

48. *Systematic Theology*, 454-55. Cf. John Murray, *The Covenant of Grace* (London: The Tyndale Press, 1956).

49. Lewis, *Robert Lewis Dabney*, 164.

50. *Systematic Theology*, 233 (on the order of the decrees). Note also his refusal to speculate in other areas of theology: ibid., 317, 320, 338-39, 340-41; *Discussions*, 1:290. Dabney explains well why he dislikes theological speculation in his critique of Hodge and Turretin on "immediate imputation" in ibid., 1:165-66:

> Nearly all Dr. Hodge's positions may be found in the ninth chapter of Turretin's Locus on Original Sin. The true verdict on this history of opinion seems to us this: that a few of the more acute and forward of the Calvinistic divines were tempted, by their love of system and symmetry of statement and over-confidence in their own logic, to excogitate the ill-starred distinction of the antecedent and gratuitous imputation. Their error here was exactly like that of the supralapsarians, who thought they could throw light and symmetry on the doctrine of the decree by assigning what they thought was the logical order of sequence to its parts. But they became "wise above that which was written." They added no light to the mystery of the decree, but they misrepresented the moral attributes of God, and provoked a crowd of natural cavils and objections. The distinction of supralapsarians and infralapsarians ought never to have been heard of. . . . So, say we, this distinction of the antecedent imputation ought never to have been drawn. . . . But the difference with Dr. Hodge seems to have been this: his love of systematizing enticed him to adopt the extreme points of his great teacher, Turretin.

51. See Dabney, *Discussions,* 3:193-94, 200-05; also his *Review of Theodosia Ernest; Or, the Heroine of Faith* (Richmond: Shepperson and Graves, 1869).

52. *Systematic Theology,* 529.

53. Ibid., 239. Dr. Morton Smith suggests with insight that Dabney's refusal to parallel the decrees of election and reprobation is like that of G. C. Berkouwer, who says, "The Gospel can be understood and preached only if balance, symmetry, and parallelism are excluded" (*Divine Election,* 202); quoted in Morton Smith, *Studies in Southern Presbyterian Theology* (Amsterdam: Jacob Van Campen, 1962), 214.

54. Dabney, *Discussions,* 1:144-45, 166-67; *Systematic Theology,* 342.

55. See Dabney, *Discussions,* 1:285-86, 307; *Systematic Theology,* 532-33, 559.

56. Ibid., 609.

57. Ibid., 163-64; also *Sensualistic Philosophy,* 324. Terrill Elniff explains the significance of this debate among the New England Puritans in *The Guise of Every Graceless Heart* (Vallectio, CA: Ross House Books, 1981).

58. Ian H. Murray, "Preface," in *Collected Writings of John Murray* (Edinburgh: The Banner of Truth Trust, 1977), 2:vii-viii.

59. See Dabney, *Discussions,* 3:240-41, where Dabney says:

> . . . this law of free volitions is the soul's own rational and appetitive nature—its *habitus.* Hence the rational free volition is not an uncaused phenomenon in the world of mind; it only arises by reason of its regular efficient, which is the subjective motive. By subjective motive is meant that complex of mental judgment as to the preferable, and subjective appetency for the object which arise together in the mind, on presentation of the object, according to the mind's own native disposition. In a word, the free volition will arise according to and because of the soul's own strongest motive; and that is the reason why it is a rational, a free, and a responsible volition. Hence we believe that such volitions are attended with full certainty—which is what we mean by moral necessity—and also with full freedom.

See also Dabney, *Systematic Theology,* 578:

> The will has its own *habitus,* regulative of all its fundamental acts, which is not a mere modification of the intelligence, but its own co-ordinate, original character; a simple, ultimate fact of the moral constitution. Hence an interaction of will and intellect. On moral and spiritual subjects the practical generalisations of the intellect are founded on the dictates of the disposition of the will.

60. See ibid., 323:

> But when we thus discriminate the faculties, we must not forget the unity and simplicity of the spirit of man. It is a monad. And, as we do not conceive of it as regenerated or sanctified by patches; so neither do we regard it as specifically

depraved by patches. Original corruption is not, specifically, the perversion of a faculty in the soul, but of the soul itself.

61. On Dick see Dabney, *Systematic Theology*, 578; on Thornwell, ibid., 298; on Hodge, ibid., 570-71 and *Discussions*, 1:232-34; on Bledsoe, *Discussions*, 3:181ff. and 211ff.

62. See *Systematic Theology*, Lecture XLVII, esp. 561-62. Cf. Thomas Boston, *Human Nature in its Fourfold State* (London: The Banner of Truth Trust, 1964), part III, "Regeneration."

63. Dabney, *Discussions*, 3:274-75.

64. In his *Practical Philosophy*, Dabney arranged the feelings in terms of pairs under nine "sensibilities." Each pair is bounded at opposite ends by desire and aversion. In light of subsequent developments in psychology before and after, pro and con Freud, Dabney's work is somewhat dated and limited in scope. Yet as ethics it still deserves a serious reading.

65. His "Love of Applause" and "Duties of the Family" are models of penetrating ethical insight, and his "Civic Duties" raises many of the most difficult critical questions that face Christians today who live under hostile regimes (see his *Practical Philosophy*).

66. See Dabney, *Discussions*, 3:456-61.

67. See ibid., 2:161-62.

68. Dabney, *Systematic Theology*, 281.

69. Ibid., 279-80.

70. Ibid., 286-91.

71. See Dabney, *Sensualistic Philosophy*, 352-69.

72. Cf. ibid., 353, 359-60. By this superintendence, God "guides with His skillful but invisible hand to just those combinations which release the powers of the second causes He needs for His purpose, and reduce to potentiality those whose tasks are for the time completed" (359-60).

73. *Systematic Theology*, 811. See also on the question of the nature of our union with Christ, 616-17, 730. Dabney wishes to refute Calvin's *Institutes*, IV, ch. 17 (*Institutes of the Christian Religion*, 2 vols., ed. John T. McNeill, trans. Ford Lewis Battles [Philadelphia: The Westminster Press, 1977]). Ronald S. Wallace's important study *Calvin's Doctrine of Word and Sacrament* (Tyler, TX: Geneva Divinity School Press, 1982, rpt.).

74. See John B. Adger, *My Life and Times, 1810-1899* (Richmond, VA: The Presbyterian Committee of Publication, 1899), 310-26.

75. See esp. David H. Overy, "When the Wicked Beareth Rule: A Southern Critique of Industrial America," *Journal of Presbyterian History* (Summer 1970), esp. 132, 135. See also David H. Overy, *Dabney: Apostle*, 290; also Dabney, *Discussions*, 4:1-24.

76. See Smylie, "The Burden of Southern Church Historians," 291; also Dabney, *The Practical Philosophy*, 476; *Discussions*, 4:53-70 and 321-40; and David H. Overy, *Dabney: Apostle*, 285-88.

77. Dabney, *Discussions*, 4:341-53.

78. Dabney, *Defence of Virginia*, 15; also Overy, "When the Wicked Beareth Rule," 135.

79. See his various articles against the Virginia state school system in *Discussions*, 4:176-247, 260-80. See also E. T. Thompson, *Presbyterians in the South*, 3 vols. (Richmond: John Knox Press, 1963-73), 2:341-49.

80. Dabney predicts in his *Practical Philosophy*, 394:

The history of human rights is, that their intelligent assertors usually learn the true grounds of them "in the furnace of affliction"; that the posterity who inherit

> these rights hold them for a while, in pride and ignorant prescription; that after a while, when the true logic of the rights has been forgotten, and when some plausible temptation presses them to do so, the next generation discards the precious rights bodily, and goes back to the practice of the old tyranny. . . .
>
> You may deem it a strange prophecy, but I predict that the time will come in this once free America when the battle for religious liberty will have to be fought over again, and will probably be lost, because the people are already ignorant of its true basis and conditions.

See also his *Discussions,* 3:321, 503.

81. See, e.g., his controversy with Professor Woodrow of Columbia Seminary, who came to accept organic evolution, in *Discussions,* 3:91-181; also *Sensualistic Philosophy,* ch. 6.

82. See Dabney, *Discussions,* 1:350-439.

83. T. C. Johnson, *Life and Letters,* 532.

84. Dabney, *Discussions,* 4:545, 3:564. In an undated letter to the Rev. R. H. Fleming of Woodstock, Virginia, Dabney speaks of the refusal of the Presbyterian General Assembly to speak against current sins, which undercuts sessional discipline, which in turn—Dabney feared—would lead "to the death of the church." This letter is in the collection of the Presbyterian Historical Foundation, Montreat, North Carolina.

85. See R. L. Dabney, *Sacred Rhetoric* (Carlisle, PA: The Banner of Truth Trust, 1979), 115-17 on unction; and Thompson, *Presbyterians in the South,* 2:429-35 on changes in worship.

86. See Dabney, *Discussions,* 2:76-95 and 551-74.

87. Dabney, *Systematic Theology,* 601.

88. See Dabney, *Discussions,* 1:1-28, 4:528; T. C. Johnson, *Life and Letters,* 408.

89. See Dabney, *Discussions,* 2:199-217; Johnson, *Life and Letters,* 319-22.

90. See Dabney, *Discussions,* 4:176-90.

91. See ibid., 25-45.

92. Ibid., 109-12.

93. Terry Johnson, "Gone with the Wind: R. L. Dabney and the Evangelical Defense of Slavery" (Paper written at Gordon-Conwell Theological Seminary), 38.

94. Johnson, *Life and Letters,* 325-26.

95. Charles R. Wilson, "Robert Lewis Dabney: Religion and the Southern Holocaust," *The Virginia Magazine of History and Biography,* 89 (January 1981), 89.

96. Overy, "When the Wicked Beareth Rule," 131.

97. Johnson, *Life and Letters,* p. 569.

3

JAMES HENLEY THORNWELL

LUDER G. WHITLOCK, JR.

Photo courtesy of Presbyterian Study Center.

James Henley Thornwell

JAMES Henley Thornwell once expressed a desire "to be regarded as the greatest scholar and most talented man that ever lived."[1] Although he failed to achieve that distinction, Thornwell did become one of the outstanding Presbyterian leaders of the nineteenth century, rising rapidly in the esteem of his colleagues, so that in 1847 at the age of 35 he became the youngest moderator of the General Assembly in the history of the Presbyterian Church in the United States. This son of a plantation overseer, as a result of a discussion about Aristotle at a dinner party in New York in 1856, received a copy of Aristotle from Harvard professor George Bancroft, who was sufficiently impressed to inscribe on the flyleaf the following words: "A testimonial of regard to the Rev. Dr. J. H. Thornwell, the most learned of the learned."[2] Daniel Webster, after hearing Thornwell speak at a South Carolina college, was reported to have remarked that he was the greatest pulpit orator he had ever heard.[3] And Henry Ward Beecher referred to him as the most brilliant minister in the Old School Presbyterian Church and the most brilliant debater in the General Assembly.[4] He was selected by the Board of Commissioners on World Missions to preach the anniversary sermon at the General Assembly in New York City in 1856. It is said that Thornwell would have been the first man pointed out to a stranger arriving at his first General Assembly. Moreover, the stranger probably would have been surprised to discover that this small, stooped gentleman so unimpressive in physical appearance was the acclaimed J. H. Thornwell.

In 1837 he was elected to the professorship of Logic and Belles Lettres at South Carolina College where he had graduated first in his class in 1831. He spent the greater part of his professional years at the college, remaining there until 1855 except for one year, 1840-41, during which period he served as the pastor of the First Presbyterian Church in Columbia, South Carolina. Thornwell had a significant influence on the college as professor, chaplain, and president. As the sixth president, he was perhaps the most important person connected with the college until that time, for in him the institution possessed the outstanding religious personality in the state and perhaps the outstanding Presbyterian in the South.[5] In 1855 his tenure as president of the college was terminated in order for him to become Professor of Didactic and Polemic Theology in the theological seminary at Columbia. This he did for the benefit of the seminary, which was at this time in a precarious position insofar as the strength of its faculty was concerned. His presence assured confidence and support for the seminary from the church.

It is not surprising to discover that when the Southern Presbyterian churches withdrew from the Presbyterian Church in the USA in 1861, Thornwell became the principal spokesman for the Presbyterian Church in the Confederate States of America. His "Address to All the Churches of Jesus Christ Throughout the Earth" was unanimously adopted by that body at its initial General Assembly at Augusta, Georgia, in December 1861.[6] It was in the Presbyterian churches of the southern states that he left his lasting mark, and that influence was strongest in the area of ecclesiology.[7] His views essentially became the position of the Presbyterian Church, U.S. for about a century and are to a large degree embodied in the recently formed Presbyterian Church in America.[8]

Ecclesiastical Debate

Thornwell's contribution must be evaluated in the light of the period in which he lived. During the first half of the nineteenth century American Presbyterians became embroiled in heated debate and serious reflection regarding their theology and church government. A primary cause of this intensive discussion was the Plan of Union of 1801, designed to bring Presbyterians and Congregationalists into close cooperation. Their common Calvinistic heritage and regular correspondence dating back to 1766 made the arrangement seem most reasonable.[9] The Plan of Union allowed new congregations to choose a minister from either denomination, to rule themselves according to Presbyterian or Congregational government, and to send official representatives to meetings of either denomination. In addition, voluntary benevolent societies were formed as a joint venture by individuals from both denominations.[10]

This period of cooperation was halted abruptly by the rupture of Presbyterians into Old and New Schools in 1837. The Old School Presbyterians had become convinced that the New England theology was diluting the confessional stance of the Westminster Confession of Faith and that the future of Presbyterianism was in jeopardy. They were evidently even more upset by their inability to control the situation.[11] Therefore, when the Old School Presbyterians found themselves holding the majority of commissioners at the 1837 General Assembly they proceeded to excise the New School Presbyterians, including all churches, presbyteries, and synods received during the period in which the Plan of Union had been in effect.[12] The same General Assembly passed a resolution declaring that the American Home Missionary Society and the American Education Society were exceedingly injurious to the peace and purity of the Presbyterian Church and urged that they no longer be allowed to operate within any of the churches in the denomination.[13]

The aftermath of the division found Old School Presbyterians seeking to identify themselves as Presbyterians in contrast to Congregationalists and other denominations. Consequently, in the year subsequent to the division and until 1860, there were prolonged, often heated, debates regarding the nature of Presbyterian polity. These debates revealed that significant matters of polity had not been thoroughly worked out by the denomination previously. While revolving around topics such as church boards, the status of the ruling elder, and related matters, these debates all centered on the location and exercise of power as that related to the genius of Presbyterianism. They should probably be seen as an expression of a desire to perpetuate the Presbyterian form of government.

Exactly what was the nature and mission of the church and what would that mean for the structure of the church?[14] If various tasks such as evangelism and ministries of mercy were eventually assumed by the voluntary societies, would this mean that the church would ultimately be left with very few functions, perhaps only worship and the administration of the sacraments? Apparently concerns of this nature troubled many Presbyterians, including Charles Hodge, who argued that Thornwell's position would compel the church to divest itself not only of boards, but seminaries, colleges, and similar institutions.[15] On the other hand, if the church were to assume responsibility for the various tasks being addressed at that time by the voluntary Christian organizations, then what organizational changes would be required in order to accomplish that effectively? That question bothered Thornwell and many of his colleagues.

Thornwell harbored intense convictions regarding the distinctiveness of Presbyterian doctrine and polity. He was convinced that the principles involved in the discussions affected the heart and soul of Presbyterianism. For these reasons he entered vigorously into the debates—debates that stretched across a span of more than twenty years and culminated with his famous encounter with Charles Hodge on the issue of the administration of missions at the 1860 General Assembly in Rochester, New York.[16]

The real issue of that debate, as Hodge himself observed, was not merely the propriety of church boards, but "what is Presbyterianism?"[17]

Thornwell claimed that the central question was the organization of the church itself.[18] He insisted that "God gave us our church government, as truly as he gave us our doctrines; and we have no more right to add to the church government, than to add to the doctrine."[19] He visualized the alternatives in this way:

> Thus, one party amongst us holds that Christ gave us the materials and principles of church-government, and has left us to shape them pretty much as we please. But the other holds that God gave us *a Church*, a constitution, laws, Presbyterys, Assemblies, Presbyters, and all the functionaries necessary to a complete organization of his kingdom upon the earth and to its effective operation; that he has revealed an order as well as a *faith*, and that as our attitude in the one case is to hear and *believe*, in the other it is hear and obey. Of one of these parties the motto is, "you may do all that the Scriptures do not forbid"; of the other, "you can do only what the Scriptures command."[20]

The Presbyterianism that Thornwell espoused reserved all power for the church courts. That power belonged to the elders or presbyters who were the rulers of the church. It was not to be vested in voluntary societies or boards that could act independently of the church in its ecclesiastical capacity. If committees or boards existed, they must be directly accountable to the General Assembly of the church.[21]

Another matter of great importance to Thornwell in regard to church government was the status of the ruling elder. Some controversy had occurred during the General Assemblies of 1842-1844 regarding whether or not ruling elders had the right to lay on hands at the ordination of ministers. The 1843 General Assembly concluded that ruling elders did not have that right.[22] The 1843 General Assembly also dealt with another pertinent matter when it ruled that a presbytery meeting could be convened and a quorum could be declared present without the presence of a ruling elder.[23]

Thornwell was convinced that if the rights of the ruling elder were slighted a "sacred hierarchy" would result in the church, and the concentration of power in the hands of the clergy occurring thereby would spell doom for Presbyterianism. He was convinced that the delicate balance of power effected through two classes of presbyters, teaching and ruling elders, could not be dispensed with without serious results for Presbyterianism as a system of government. Moreover, presbyters could not be limited to the clergy, for that would be prelacy. Rather, presbyters were both ruling elders and teaching elders, that is, both laymen and clergy. "Presbyterianism stands or falls with a distinction between ruling and teaching elders," he maintained.[24] In this way the balance of power was maintained within the church courts, and this power was representative, not by proxy, which would be Congregationalism. So power was reserved for the church "in its ecclesiastical capacity," and yet that power was carefully distributed between clergy and laity acting in a representative capacity. In that way he distinguished Presbyterianism from every other form of church government:

> The government of the Church by parliamentary assemblies, composed of two classes of Elders, and of Elders only and so arranged to realize the visible unity of the whole church—this is Presbyterianism.[25]

Since differing views on theology and church government were the principal issues leading to the division of 1837 and, with the slavery issue, continued to dominate the attention of Presbyterians during the remainder of Thornwell's life, it is not surprising that a major portion of his energies was directed to these matters.[26]

Invariably, his immediate recourse for the resolution of the matter was to the authoritative Scriptures. In this respect he found company with Old School Presbyterians and other evangelical Christians of his era. His basic assumption in developing his arguments was the hermeneutical principle that whatever is not commanded in the Bible is forbidden. There would have been a consensus among many of his colleagues in regard to this principle as well. Thornwell is open to criticism, however, for his failure to justify this hermeneutical principle so crucial to the development of his argument. Thornwell's difficulty lay not in the persuasive power of his vigorous logical mind, but rather in a failure to plumb carefully and vigorously the assumptions on which he built his telling arguments.

Another question that comes to mind as one assesses his involvement in the discussions on church government is the degree to which the secular political situation may have influenced Thornwell and his contemporaries in the divergent approaches toward the polity that they adopted. For example, the states'-rights principles that became important factors in southern sectionalism appear to be reflected somewhat in the Thornwellian polity. Perhaps this is the explanation for Thornwell's desire to retain as much authority as possible for presbyteries, especially if it is kept in mind that Thornwell was from South Carolina where southern sentiments were most pronounced and which was also the home state of John C. Calhoun, formulator of the doctrine of nullification. This might also partially explain the keen interest of Southern Presbyterians to maintain a balance of power though the parity of elders since Southerners were sensitive to such matters because of their efforts to maintain a balance of power in Congress as more states were added, both slave and free, and as the population of the northern states swelled more rapidly, yielding them an edge in the House of Representatives. The question is not one of Thornwell's theological integrity, nor that of Southern Presbyterians in general; rather, it is the question to what degree one remains captive to his culture while attempting to understand and apply the truth of the Bible.

Similar questions may be raised regarding Thornwell's position on slavery. He was well aware of the magnitude and pervasiveness of this issue. In his opinion, the Bible did not condemn slavery and so the church should not do so either. Actually, Thronwell concluded,

> The Scriptures not only fail to condemn slavery, they as distinctly sanction it as any other social condition of man. The Church was formally organized in the family of a slaveholder; the relation was divinely regulated among the chosen people of God; and the peculiar duties of the parties are inculcated under the Christian economy. These are facts which cannot be denied.[27]

If that was the case, then Christians needed to the fullest extent possible to bring biblical principles to bear on all aspects of the current practice of slavery. So Thornwell developed a position for a Christian doctrine of slavery that included a careful delineation of the status of the slave as a person made in the image of God and therefore as one who should be regarded as a brother.[28] The master did not have a right to unlimited control, but only a right to his labor.[29] On the other hand, Thornwell argued that if a master should emancipate his slave, then operating on the same benevolent principle a rich man should share all of his estate with his poor neighbors. If such ideas were implemented it would, he warned, bring disaster to all institutions of civilized society.[30]

Scripture and Philosophy

A more reasonable explanation for Thornwell's positions than the influence of the political situation seems to be the influence of Scottish Common Sense Philosophy, resulting in a cultural and social conservativism that typified the views of James Henley Thornwell and Old School Presbyterians.[31] Scottish Common Sense Philosophy dominated Princetonian thought from Witherspoon on and Old School Presbyterianism throughout the first half of the nineteenth century. Princeton was by far the most influential of the northern colleges on southern education.[32] Therefore, it is relatively easy to see how Common Sense Philosophy would have become pervasive in the South. Southern colleges offered courses in moral philosophy, required of all students, introducing Scottish Common Sense Philosophy to them in this manner.[33] This school of philosophy not only became dominant in Old School Presbyterianism, but became "The Reliable Handmaiden of Southern Theology,"[34] and Thornwell was no exception to the rule. There is the specific reason that Robert Henry, Professor of Logic and Ethics at South Carolina College, had studied at Edinburgh. It was said of him that he was the man who had taught South Carolinians to think. Henry, Thornwell's professor, introduced him to Dugald Stuart's writings, and Thornwell read them before moving on to the study of William Hamilton.[35]

Thornwell warmly embraced this mode of thinking, as can be seen from his writings.[36] In his inaugural address as professor at Columbia Theological Seminary, he noted that the task of theological scholarship was to show the complete harmony of sound philosophy and theology.[37] He saw the truth of nature and Scripture in harmony, and he saw them as one system of truth. Since grace presupposed nature, there was a need to lay the natural foundation for an examination of the Scriptures. To begin abruptly with the doctrine of redemption with no connection to natural religion did not appeal to him at all.[38] Thornwell saw moral philosophy as a form of natural theology and the ground of moral obligation to be through philosophical description. Although ethics was based on biblical precept, actually the Scriptures were a validation of the conclusions of Common Sense Philosophy.[39]

That this should be the case seems incongruous with Thornwell's insistence on the final, determinative authority of the Scriptures for faith and practice. His statements regarding this matter are unequivocal:

> Christianity in its living principles and its outward forms is purely a matter of Divine revelation. The great error of the Church in all ages, the fruitful source of her apostasy and crime, has been a presumptuous reliance upon her own understanding. Her own inventions have seduced her from her loyalty to God, and filled her sanctuary with idols and the hearts of her children with vain imaginations. The Bible cuts at the very root of this evil by affording us a perfect and infallible rule of faith and practice. The absolute perfection of the Scriptures as a directory to man was a cardinal principle of the Reformation, and whatever could not be traced to them either directly or by necessary inference was denounced as a human invention—as mere will-worship, which God abhors so deeply that an inspired Apostle has connected it with idolatry or the worshipping of angels.[40]

Of course, there is no question about his desire to be faithful to the Scriptures and for them to serve as his ultimate authority. The question is rather to what degree he was able to achieve this objective as a theologian. In answering this question, the influence of Common Sense Philosophy on his theology must be measured carefully. An evaluation of Old School Presbyterianism and Princeton theology appears to be equally applicable to Thornwell:

> In short, what is praiseworthy in this Presbyterian theology is its eagerness to be confessionally scriptural, scientifically respectable, and culturally relevant. It made a valiant attempt to retain its theological orthodoxy while it was constantly surrounded, and at times subtly tempted, by formidable philosophical movements that seemed, outwardly, at least, to be congenial to a biblical stance.
>
> This desire to be fully biblical was so strong that these Presbyterian theologians soon developed the conviction that all their ideas, including the philosophical, were of a thoroughly scriptural character, as well as the belief that their reading and understanding of Scripture was not in any way blurred by superimposed philosophical constructs.
>
> It could be maintained that the scriptural intent of Presbyterian theology has actually been undermined by the attempts of this theology, particularly during the nineteenth century, to adapt itself to certain philosophical thought-patterns that were then culturally in vogue. In fact, these philosophical ideas were generally neither expressive of, nor congenial to, a full-orbed, scriptural ontology, anthropology, and epistemology.[41]

Thornwell's affirmation of Common Sense Philosophy invariably led him to a particular view of the sinful world in which he lived and how that world could best be brought into conformity to the Bible. In the first place, he accepted society with all its imperfections as the consequence of God's providential ordering of things.[42] He viewed society and nature as joint aspects of a whole—one unified scheme. Society involved a system of relationships rooted in natural law. Therefore, just as growth and development were slow, gradual processes in nature, in similar fashion one would anticipate that that would be the case with God's design for progress and reform in society; one would not expect it to involve "sudden changes or violent revolutions."[43] The influence of believing individuals would be an appropriate catalyst for salutary change.

This attitude toward social change sounds somewhat similar to but is different from Thornwell's view of the "spirituality of the church."[44] Attributed to Thornwell, this position was a distinctive of Southern Presbyterianism for many years. Essentially, he delineated two separate spheres of authority and function: the church and the state were "as planets moving in different orbits."[45] The church, he said,

> is exclusively a spiritual organization, . . . she has nothing to do with the voluntary associations of men for various social and civic purposes. . . . Her mission is to bring men to the cross, to reconcile them to God . . . imbue them with the spirit of the Divine Master

> and then send them forth to perform their social duties, to manage society, and perform the functions that pertain to their social and civic relations.[46]

The church was limited in the scope of its activity. It was not to interfere with the state and its decisions. But the individual Christian experienced no such restriction. He was expected to be active, and the more Christians who participated in government, the more Thornwell would have been pleased. He was active himself, drafting a paper on slavery, advocating support of public schools and the inclusion of religious instruction in the curriculum, and shaping a General Assembly statement regarding peace in Mexico. Occasionally the relationships appear to be blurred as, for example, when he joined the Synod of South Carolina in urging the people of South Carolina "to imitate their revolutionary forefathers and stand up for their rights."[47] In holding this position regarding church and state, Thornwell placed himself in the tradition of the Westminster Confession of Faith.

Conclusion

Thornwell must be viewed as a champion of his Old School Presbyterian theological heritage. His forceful, eloquent leadership contributed substantially toward assuring a legacy of orthodoxy for later generations of Southern Presbyterians. His desire to understand the Scriptures and to seek obedient conformity to them in church and society is the essence of what it means to be Reformed. His weakness lay in assuming that his understanding of the Scriptures was not distorted by his philosophical frame of reference, which was weak in regard to the relationship between natural and revealed theology. Thus his remarkable contribution bears the theological and philosophical marks of the nineteenth-century Old School Presbyterian mold in which it was cast.

James Henley Thornwell still casts a long shadow in Southern Presbyterianism, particularly in the nascent Presbyterian Church in America and in the Reformed Theological Seminary in Jackson, Mississippi.

Notes: James Henley Thornwell

1. Benjamin Morgan Palmer, *Life and Letters of James Henley Thornwell* (Richmond: Whittet and Shepperson, 1875), 397.
2. Ibid., 537.
3. Paul L. Garber, "James Henley Thornwell: Presbyterian Defender of the Old South," *Union Seminary Review* 54 (February 1943): 99.
4. Ibid.

5. Daniel W. Hollis, *The University of South Carolina*, 2 vols. (Columbia, SC: University of South Carolina Press, 1951), 1:161.

6. The address provided the rationale for the establishment of the Presbyterian Church in the Confederate States of America.

7. Thomas Peck, a contemporary, thought Thornwell's great contribution was in ecclesiology (Thomas E. Peck, *Miscellanies of Rev. Thomas E. Peck*, ed. T. C. Johnson, 3 vols. [Richmond: The Presbyterian Committee of Publication, 1895], 1:434). Garber, "In whatever manner the Southern Presbyterian church may have departed from the ideals he defined for its establishment in 1861, that denomination remains to an extent the lengthened shadow of James Henley Thornwell as the Scottish church is of John Knox" (Garber, "Thornwell," 99). H. Sheldon Smith concluded that Thornwell's theological thought dominated most of the history of Southern Presbyterianism ("The Church and the Social Order in the Old South as Interpreted by James H. Thornwell," *Church History* 7 [June 1938]: 115ff.).

8. The First General Assembly of the Presbyterian Church in America met in Birmingham, Alabama, on December 4, 1973. The name National Presbyterian Church was selected at this initial assembly, but changed at the 1974 General Assembly.

9. William O. Bracket, Jr., "The Rise and Development of the New School in the Presbyterian Church in the USA to the Reunion of 1869," *The Journal of the Presbyterian Historical Society* 13:121.

10. The American Home Missionary Society and the American Board of Commissioners for Foreign Missions were two of the societies that functioned under the Plan of Union. Tension soon began to rise, however, because of increasing denominational interests in the official boards and agencies of the Presbyterian Church. Cf. Clifford S. Griffin, "Cooperation in Conflict: The Schism in the American Home Missionary Society, 1837-1861," *Journal of the Presbyterian Historical Society* 28 (1960): 213-233.

11. George M. Marsden, *The Evangelical Mind and the New School Presbyterian Experience* (New Haven: Yale University Press, 1970), 59.

12. Approximately half of the denomination was ejected by this action, which eliminated about 100,000 members.

13. This development was not peculiar to Presbyterians alone. Similar efforts emphasizing denominational distinctives were occurring in several major ecclesiastical bodies during the first half of the nineteenth century. This would be expected in the light of the numerical and geographical expansion that was occurring.

14. For samples of recent literature that has grappled with the relationship of church and parachurch groups as well as the structure of the church itself, see Richard G. Hutchenson, Jr., *Mainline Churches and the Evangelicals: A Challenging Crisis* (Atlanta: John Knox Press, 1981); also Hutchenson, *Wheel Within the Wheel: Confronting the Management Crisis of the Pluralistic Church* (Atlanta: John Knox Press, 1979); Howard A. Snyder, *The Problem of Wineskins: Church Structure in a Technological Age* (Downers Grove: InterVarsity Press, 1975); Ralph D. Winter, "The Two Structures of God's Redemptive Mission," in *American Society of Missiology* (1974).

15. *The Collected Writings of James Henley Thornwell* ed. John B. Adger and John L. Girardeau, 4 vols. (Richmond, VA: Presbyterian Committee of Publication, 1871-1881), 1:230-31.

16. For a more detailed account of Thornwell's views on this subject see

Kenneth J. Foreman, Jr., "The Debate on the Administration of Missions by James Henley Thornwell in the Presbyterian Church 1839-1861" (Ph.D. diss., Princeton University, 1977). For a more comprehensive analysis of Thornwell's views see Morton H. Smith, *Studies in Southern Presbyterian Theology* (Jackson, MS: Presbyterian Reformation Society, 1962), 121-82.

17. Charles Hodge, "Presbyterianism," *Biblical Repertory and Princeton Review* 32 (October 8, 1860): 546.

18. Adger and Girardeau, eds., *Collected Writings,* 4:218.

19. Ibid.

20. Ibid.

21. Ibid., 230.

22. *Minutes of a General Assembly of the Presbyterian Church in the USA, 1838-1847* (Philadelphia: Presbyterian Board of Publication and Sabbath School work, n.d.), 276-77.

23. Ibid.

24. Adger and Girardeau, eds., *Collected Writings,* 125.

25. Ibid., 267. It is interesting to note that in the infant Presbyterian Church in the Confederate States of America, Thornwell's position was adopted and the parity of ruling elders and teaching elders was closely guarded. See Ernest T. Thompson, *Presbyterians in the South,* 3 vols. (Richmond: John Knox Press, 1963), 1:516. For an analysis of Thornwell's position on the parity of elders see Luder G. Whitlock, Jr., "Elders and Ecclesiology in the Thought of James Henley Thornwell," *Westminster Theological Journal* 38 (Fall 1974): 44.

26. Lefferts Loetscher, *The Broadening Church* (Philadelphia: University of Pennsylvania Press, 1957), 5; Marsden, *The Evangelical Mind and the New School Presbyterian Experience,* 67.

27. Adger and Girardeau, eds., *Collected Writings,* 4:386-87.

28. Ibid., 403.

29. Thornwell, "The State of the Country," *Southern Presbyterian Review* 13:874.

30. Ibid., 391, 432. Also see H. Shelton Smith, "The Church and the Social Order in the Old South as Interpreted by James H. Thornwell," *Church History* 7 (June 1938): 115-24.

31. An excellent presentation of this point of view is found in Theodore Dwight Bozeman, "Science, Nature, and Society: A New Approach to James Henley Thornwell," *Journal of Presbyterian History* 50 (1972): 307-25; see also Bozeman, *Protestants in an Age of Science: The Baconian Ideal and Antebellum American Religious Thought* (Chapel Hill, NC: University of North Carolina Press, 1977); Loetscher, *The Broadening Church,* 6; V. L. Parrington, *Main Currents in American Thought,* 2 (New York: Harcourt Brace Jovanovich, 1955); D. H. Meyer, *The Instructed Conscience: The Shaping of the American National Ethic* (Philadelphia: University of Pennsylvania Press, 1972); E. Brooks Holifield, *The Gentleman Theologians: American Theology and Southern Culture, 1795-1860* (Durham, NC: Duke University Press, 1978), 110-54.

32. Donald R. Come, "The Influence of Princeton on Higher Education in the South before 1825," *William and Mary Quarterly,* third series, 2 (1945).

33. Holifield, *Gentleman Theologians,* 119.

34. Ibid., 126.

35. Dugald Stuart was a disciple of Thomas Reid at Edinburgh. This phil-

osophical frame of reference was Thornwell's heritage and milieu. Thornwell became, as might be expected, an enthusiastic advocate of the Common Sense Philosophy.

36. For a good synopsis see Bozeman, "Science, Nature, and Society"; also Holifield, *Gentleman Theologians,* 110, 126.

37. Adger and Girardeau, eds., *Collected Writings,* 1:580.

38. Ibid.

39. Holifield, *Gentleman Theologians,* 127.

40. Adger and Girardeau, eds., *Collected Writings,* 4:163-64.

41. John C. Vander Stelt, *Philosophy and Scripture: A Study in Old Princeton and Westminster Theology* (Marlton, NJ: Mack Publishing Company, 1978), 304-05, provides a very helpful survey and extensive critique.

42. Adger and Girardeau, eds., *Collected Writings,* 4:404, 421, 430.

43. Ibid., 428, 431-32.

44. See Ernest Trice Thompson, *The Spirituality of the Church* (Richmond: John Knox Press, 1961); also his *Presbyterians in the South,* Vol. 1; Bozeman, in "Science, Nature, and Society," explains his view in the light of Common Sense Philosophy, which would have disdained meddling with God's providentially ordered affairs. Adam Smith developed his *laissez-faire* economic policy out of similar philosophical principles, Bozeman notes. Is it possible that Thornwell has developed a theological equivalent? Bozeman observes that McCosh in his *Divine Government* adopts a similar pattern of reasoning. Challenging these points of view is Jack P. Maddex, "From Theocracy to Spirituality: The Southern Presbyterian Reversal on Church and State," *Journal of Presbyterian History* 54 (Winter 1976): 438-57. Maddex contends that antebellum Southern Presbyterians did not teach absolute separation of church and state.

45. Adger and Girardeau, eds., *Collected Writings,* 4:177.

46. Ibid., 473.

47. Thompson, *Presbyterians in the South,* 1:558. Thompson notes that the synod, after careful study by some of its members, concluded that a sacred inheritance of rights, as in their case, could not be surrendered without sinning against God. Therefore, this particular action must be evaluated in that light.

BIBLIOGRAPHY

1. Theologians of Southern Presbyterianism

Archibald Alexander (1772–1851)

Alexander, Archibald. *Biographical Sketches of the Founder, and Principal Alumni of the Log College*. Princeton, NJ: J. T. Robinson, 1845.

_____. *A Brief Compendium of Bible Truth*. Philadelphia: Presbyterian Board of Publication, 1846.

_____. *Christ's Gracious Invitation to the Labouring and Heavy Laden*. Philadelphia: Presbyterian Board of Publication, 1837.

_____. *Evidences of the Authenticity, Inspiration, and Canonical Authority of the Holy Scriptures*. New York: Arno, 1972.

_____. *A History of the Israelite Nation, From Their Origin to Their Dispersion at the Destruction of Jerusalem by the Romans*. Philadelphia: Martien, 1853.

_____. *Outlines of Moral Science*. New York: Charles Scribner's Sons, 1852.

_____. *Practical Sermons: To Be Read in Families and Social Meetings*. Philadelphia: Presbyterian Board of Publication, 1850?

_____. *Practical Truths. By the Rev. Archibald Alexander . . . Consisting of His Various Writings for the American Tract Society, and Correspondence from the Society's Formation in 1825, to His Death in 1851*. New York: American Tract Society, 1857.

_____. "'The Rev. William Graham,' An Address Delivered Before the Alumni Association of Washington College, VA, June 29, 1843." *Watchman of the South* VII (January 4, 1844): 78.

_____. *Suggestions in Vindication of Sunday Schools: But More Especially for the Improvement of Sunday School Books and the Enlargement of the Plan of Instruction*. Philadelphia, 1829.

_____. *Theories of the Will in the History of Philosophy*. New York: Charles Scribner's Sons, 1898.

_____. *Thoughts on Religious Experience. To Which Is Added an Appendix, Containing*

"Letters to the Aged." Philadelphia: Presbyterian Board of Publication, 1841. Reprint. Banner of Truth, 1978.

_____. *A Treatise on Justification by Faith.* Philadelphia: Presbyterian Tract and Sunday School Society, 1837.

Daniel Baker (1791–1857)

Baker, Daniel. *Revival Sermons.* Introduction by William M. Baker. Philadelphia: Martien, 1878.

Robert Lewis Breckinridge (1800–1871)

Breckinridge, Robert Lewis. *Addresses Delivered at the Inauguration of the Professors, in the Danville Theological Seminary.* Pamphlet, October 13, 1853.

_____. *Discussion on American Slavery Between George Thompson, Esq., Agent of the British and Foreign Society for the Abolition of Slavery Throughout the World and Rev. R. J. Breckinridge.* Boston, 1836.

_____. *Fidelity in Our Lot.* Pamphlet, 1855.

_____. *Knowledge of God, Objectively Considered, Being the First Part of Theology Considered as a Science of Positive Truth, Both Inductive and Deductive. . . .* New York: Carter and Brothers, 1858.

_____. *Knowledge of God, Subjectively Considered, Being the Second Part of Theology Considered as a Science of Positive Truth, Both Inductive and Deductive. . . .* New York: Carter and Brothers, 1859.

Robert Lewis Dabney (1820–1898)

Dabney, Robert Lewis. *Christ Our Penal Substitute.* Richmond, VA: Presbyterian Committee of Publication, 1898. Reprint. Harrisonburg, VA: Sprinkle, 1985.

_____. *The Christian Sabbath: Its Nature, Design and Proper Observance by the Rev. R. L. Dabney. . . .* Philadelphia: Presbyterian Board of Publication, 1882.

_____. *Discussions, Evangelical and Theological.* Richmond, VA: Presbyterian Committee of Publication, 1890–1892. Reprint. London: Banner of Truth Trust, 1967–1982.

_____. *The Doctrinal Contents of the Confession: Its Fundamental and Regulative Ideas, and the Necessity and Value of Creeds.* Richmond, VA: Presbyterian Committee of Publication, 1897. Reprint. *The Westminster Confession and Creeds.* Dallas: Presbyterian Heritage, 1983.

_____. *The Five Points of Calvinism.* Richmond, VA: Presbyterian Committee of Publication, 1895.

_____. *The Practical Philosophy, Being the Philosophy of the Feelings, of the Will, and of the Conscience, with the Ascertainment of Particular Rights and Duties.* Kansas City, MO: Hudson, Kimberly, 1897.

_____. *Sacred Rhetoric; or a Course of Lectures on Preaching. Delivered in the Union Theological Seminary of the General Assembly of the Presbyterian Church in the U.S., in Prince Edward, VA.* Richmond, VA: Presbyterian Committee of Publication,

1870.
_____. *The Sensualistic Philosophy of the Nineteenth Century, Considered.* New York: Randolph, 1875.
_____. *Syllabus and Notes of the Course of Systematic and Polemic Theology Taught in Union Theological Seminary, Virginia.* Richmond, VA: Presbyterian Committee of Publication, 1871. Reprint. *Lectures in Systematic Theology.* Grand Rapids: Zondervan, 1972.

Samuel Davies (1723–1761)

Davies, Samuel. *Charity and Truth United; or, the Way of the Multitude Exposed in Six Letters to the Rev. Mr. William Stith, A. M. President of William and Mary College.* Edited by Thomas Clinton Pears, Jr. Philadelphia: General Assembly of the Presbyterian Church in the USA, 1941.
_____. *Collected Poems.* Edited, with an introduction and notes, by Richard Beale Davis. Gainesville, FL: Scholars Facsimiles and Reprints, 1968.
_____. *The Curse of Cowardice: A Sermon Preached to the Militia of Hanover County, Virginia, at a General Muster, May 8, 1758. With a View to Raise a Company for Captain Samuel Meredith.* London: Woodbridge, 1759.
_____. *The Duty of Christians to Propagate Their Religion Among Heathens, Earnestly Recommended to the Masters of Negro Slaves in Virginia. A Sermon Preached in Hanover, January 8, 1757.* London, 1758.
_____. *Letters from the Rev. Samuel Davies, Showing the State of Religion (Particularly Among the Negroes) in Virginia. Likewise an Extract of a Letter from a Gentleman in London to His Friend in the Country, Being Some Observations of the Foregoing.* London, 1759.
_____. *Religion and Patriotism: The Constituents of a Good Soldier. A Sermon Preached to Captain Overton's Independent Company of Volunteers, Raised in Hanover County, Virginia, Aug. 17, 1755.* Philadelphia: James Chattin, 1755.
_____. *Religion and the Public Spirit. A Valedictory Address to the Senior Class, Delivered in Nassau-Hall, September 21, 1760, the Sunday Before Commencement.* New York: William Bradford, 1761.
_____. *The Reverend Samuel Davies Abroad; the Diary of a Journey to England and Scotland, 1753-55.* Edited, with an introduction, by George William Pilcher. Urbana, IL: University of Illinois Press, 1967.
_____. *A Sermon Delivered at Nassau-Hall, January 14, 1761, On the Death of His Late Majesty King George II.* New York: William Bradford, 1761.
_____. *Sermons on Important Subjects, By the Late Reverend and Pious Samuel Davies . . . 5th ed. . . . To Which Are Now Added, Three Occasional Sermons, Not Included in the Former Editions, Memoirs and Character of the Author, and Two Sermons on Occasion of His Death, by the Rev. Drs. Gibbons and Finley. . . .* Edited by Albert Barnes. New York: Carter and Brothers, 1853.
_____. *The State of Religion Among the Protestant Dissenters in Virginia.* Boston: Kneeland, 1951.
_____. *Virginia's Danger and Remedy: Two Discourses Occasioned by the Severe Drought*

in Sundry Parts of the Country; and the Defeat of General Braddock. Williamsburg, VA: Hunter, 1956.

John Lafayette Girardeau (1825–1898)

Girardeau, John Lafayette. *Calvinism and Evangelical Arminianism: Compared as to Election, Reprobation, Justification, and Related Doctrines.* Columbia, SC: Duffie; New York: Baker and Taylor, 1890.

_____. *Discussions of Philosophical Questions.* Edited by George A. Blackburn. Richmond, VA: Presbyterian Committee of Publication, 1900.

_____. *Discussions of Theological Questions.* Edited by George A. Blackburn. Richmond, VA: Presbyterian Committee of Publication, 1905.

_____. *Instrumental Music in the Public Worship of the Church.* Richmond, VA: Whittet and Shepperson, 1888.

_____. *Sermons.* Edited by George A. Blackburn under the auspices of the synods of South Carolina, Georgia, Alabama, and Florida. Columbia, SC: State Company, 1907.

_____. *Theology as Science Involving an Inaugural Address.* Columbia, SC: Presbyterian Publication House, 1876. Reproduced in microform, Chicago: American Theological Library Association, 1985.

_____. *The Will in Its Theological Relations.* Columbia, SC: Duffie; New York: Baker and Taylor, 1891.

Moses Drury Hoge (1819–1899)

Hoge, Moses Drury. "The Day of Adversity." *Sermons Selected from the Manuscripts.* Richmond, VA: Pollard, 1821.

_____. *The Perfection of Beauty, and Other Sermons by the Rev. Moses D. Hoge . . . with a Lecture on "The Success of Christianity an Evidence of Its Divine Origin," Delivered at the University of Virginia.* Richmond, VA: Presbyterian Committee of Publication, 1904.

_____. *Sermons Selected from the Manuscripts of the Late Moses Hoge, D.D.* Richmond, VA: Pollard, 1821.

_____. "The Sofists Unmasked; in a Series of Letters, Addressed to Thomas Paine, Author of a Book, Entitled *The Age of Reason.*" In R. Watson, *Christian Panoply; Containing an Apology for the Bible.* Richmond: Union Theological Seminary in Virginia, 1797.

_____. *Strictures upon a Pamphlet Lately Published by Jeremiah Walker: Titled "The Fourfold Foundation of Calvinism Examined and Shaken."* Philadelphia: Young, 1792.

George Howe (1802–1883)

Howe, George. *An Appeal to the Young Men of the Presbyterian Church in the Synod of South Carolina and Georgia.* Columbia, SC: Theological Seminary, 1836.

_____. *A Discourse on Theological Education; Delivered on the Bicentenary of the Westminster Assembly of Divines, July, 1843. To Which Is Added, Advice to a Student*

Preparing for the Ministry. New York: Leavitt, Trow and Co., 1844.
_____. *History of the Presbyterian Church in South Carolina*. Columbia: Duffie and Chapman, 1870–83.

Charles Colcock Jones (1804–1863)

Jones, Charles Colcock. *A Catechism of Scripture Doctrine and Practice for Families and Sabbath Schools Designed also for the Oral Instruction of Colored Persons*. Charleston: Harrison, 1845.
_____. *A Georgian at Princeton*. Edited by Robert Manson Myers. New York: Harcourt Brace Jovanovich, 1976.
_____. *The Children of Pride: Selected Letters of the Family of the Rev. Dr. Charles Colcock Jones for the Years 1860–1868, with the Addition of Several Previously Unpublished Letters*. Edited by Robert Manson Myers. New Haven: Yale University Press, 1984.
_____. *The Religious Instruction of the Negroes in the United States*. Savannah: Purse, 1842.

John Leland (1754–1841)

Leland, John. *The Writings of the Late Elder John Leland, Including Some Events in His Life, Written by Himself*. Edited by L.F. Green. New York, 1845.

Benjamin Morgan Palmer (1818–1902)

Palmer, Benjamin Morgan. *The Broken Home; or, Lessons in Sorrow*. 2d ed. New Orleans: Upton, 1891.
_____. *The Family in Its Civil and Churchly Aspects: An Essay in Two Parts*. Harrisonburg, VA: Sprinkle, 1981.
_____. *Formation of Character. Twelve Lectures Delivered in the First Presbyterian Church, New Orleans, LA*. New Orleans: Religious Book Depository, 1889.
_____. "Life, Character, and Genius of the Late Rev. James Henley Thornwell, D.D., LL.D." *Southern Presbyterian Review* 15 (October 1862): 255–309.
_____. *The Life and Letters of James Henley Thornwell: Ex-president of the South Carolina College, Late Professor of Theology in the Theological Seminary at Columbia, South Carolina*. Richmond, VA: Whittet and Shepperson, 1875. Reprint. London: Banner of Truth Trust, 1974.
_____. *The Pious Physician; or, The Claims of Religion upon the Medical Profession*. Richmond, VA: Presbyterian Committee on Publication, 1871.
_____. "The Proposed Plan of Union Between the General Assembly of the Presbyterian Church in the Confederate States of America and the United Synod of the South." *Southern Presbyterian Review* 16 (April 1864): 264–307.
_____. *The South: Her Peril, and Her Duty: A Discourse, Delivered in the First Presbyterian Church, New Orleans, on Thursday, November 29, 1860*. New Orleans: Office of the True Witness and Sentinel, 1860.
_____. *Theology of Prayer: as Viewed in the Religion of Nature and in the System of Grace*.

Richmond, VA: Presbyterian Committee of Publication, 1894. Reprint. Harrisonburg, VA: Sprinkle, 1980.

_____. "Thornwell's Writings." *Southern Presbyterian Review* 29 (July 1878): 413–48.

_____. *The Threfold Fellowship and the Threefold Assurance: An Essay in Two Parts.* Richmond, VA: Presbyterian Committee of Publication, 1902.

_____. *A Weekly Publication Containing Sermons by Rev. B. M. Palmer.* 2 vols. Reported by C.W. Colton. New Orleans: Clark and Hofeline, 1875–1876.

Thomas Ephraim Peck, D.D., LL.D. (1822–1893)

Peck, T. E. *Miscellanies of Rev. Thomas E. Peck, D.D., LL.D., Professor of Theology in the Union Theological Seminary in Virginia.* 2 vols. Edited by Rev. T. C. Johnson. Richmond, VA: Presbyterian Committee of Publication, 1895.

_____. *Notes on Ecclesiology.* Richmond, VA: Presbyterian Committee of Publication, 1892.

David Rice (1733–1816)

Rice, David. *A Lecture on the Divine Decrees, to Which Is Annexed a Few Observations on a Piece Lately Printed in Lexington, Entitled "the Principles of the Methodists, or the Scripture Doctrine of Pre-Destination, Election and Reprobation."* Lexington, KY: John Bradford, 1791.

_____. *A Sermon on the Present Revival of Religion, etc., in This Country; Preached at the Opening of the Kentucky Synod.* Lexington, KY: Joseph Charles, 1803.

_____. *Slavery Inconsistent with Justice and Good Policy, Proved by a Speech, Delivered in the Convention Held at Danville, Kentucky.* Philadelphia, 1804.

John Holt Rice (1818–1878)

Rice, John Holt. *Discourse Delivered Before the General Assembly of the Presbyterian Church in the United States of America on the Opening of Their Session, in 1820.* Philadelphia: Thomas and William Bradford, 1820.

Samuel Stanhope Smith (1750–1819)

Smith, Samuel Stanhope. *An Essay on the Causes of the Variety of Complexion and Figure in the Human Species.* 2d ed., 1810. Reprint. Edited, with an introduction, by Winthrop D. Jordan. Cambridge: Belknap, 1965.

_____. *The Lectures, Corrected and Improved, Which Have Been Delivered for a Series of Years, in the College of New Jersey; on the Subjects of Moral and Political Philosophy.* Trenton, 1812.

Thomas Smyth (1808–1873)

Smyth, Thomas. *Complete Works of Rev. Thomas Smyth, D.D.* Edited by J. William Flinn. 10 vols. Columbia, SC: Bryan, 1908.

James Henley Thornwell (1812–1862)

Thornwell, James Henley. *The Collected Writings of James Henley Thornwell, D.D., LL.D.: Late Professor of Theology in the Theological Seminary at Columbia, South Carolina.* Edited by John B. Adger. Richmond, VA: Presbyterian Committee of Publication, 1871.

_____. *Discourses on Truth: Delivered in the Chapel of the South Carolina College.* New York: Carter, 1854.

_____. *Election and Reprobation.* Jackson, MS: Presbyterian Reformation Society, 1961.

_____. "Slavery and the Religious Instruction of the Colored Population." *Southern Presbyterian Review* 4 (1850): 126–28.

Robert Alexander Webb (1856–1919)

Webb, Robert Alexander. *Christian Salvation, Its Doctrine and Experience, by Robert Alexander Webb. . . .* Richmond, VA: Presbyterian Committee of Publication, 1921. Reprint. Harrisonburg, VA: Sprinkle, 1985.

_____. *The Reformed Doctrine of Adoption.* Grand Rapids: Eerdmans, 1947.

_____. *The Theology of Infant Salvation.* Richmond, VA: Presbyterian Committee of Publication, 1907. Reprint. Harrisonburg, VA: Sprinkle, 1981.

Collected Works

Memorial Volume of the Semi-Centennial of the Theological Seminary at Columbia, South Carolina. Columbia, SC: Presbyterian Publishing House, 1884.

Southern Presbyterian Pulpit: A Collection of Sermons by Ministers of the Southern Presbyterian Church. Richmond, VA: Presbyterian Committee of Publication, 1896.

2. Presbyterian Church in the United States: History and Theology

Adger, John B. "James Henley Thornwell, D.D., LL.D." *Memorial Volume of the Semi-Centennial of the Theological Seminary at Columbia, South Carolina.* Columbia, SC: Presbyterian Publishing House, 1884.

Adger, John B., and Girardeau, John L., eds. *The Collected Writings of James Henley Thornwell, D.D. LL.D.* 4 vols. Richmond, VA: Presbyterian Committee of Publication, 1871–1873.

Alexander, James W. *The Life of Archibald Alexander, C.C., First Professor in the Theological Seminary, at Princeton, New Jersey.* New York: Charles Scribner's Sons, 1854.

_____. "The Rev. Jas. Waddel, D.D." *Watchman of the South* 7 (March 28, 1844): 126, 134, 138.

Alley, Robert S. *The Reverend Mr. Samuel Davies: A Study in Religion and Politics, 1747–1759.* Ph.D. diss., Princeton University, 1962.

Baldwin, Alice M. "Sowers of Sedition: The Political Theories of Some of the New

Light Presbyterian Clergy of Virginia and North Carolina." *William and Mary Quarterly* 3d series, 5 (January 1948): 52–76.

Baker, William M. *The Life and Labours of the Rev. Daniel Baker, D.D. Pastor and Evangelist.* Philadelphia: Martien, 1858.

Blackburn, George A., ed. *The Life Work of John L. Girardeau, D.D., LL.D., Late Professor of the Presbyterian Theological Seminary, Columbia, S.C.* Columbia, SC: State Company, 1916.

Bost, George H. *"Samuel Davies" Colonial Revivalist and Champion of Religious Toleration.* Ph.D. diss., University of Chicago, 1959.

Bozeman, Theodore Dwight. *A Nineteenth-Century Baconian Theology: James Henley Thornwell as Enlightenment Theologian.* Th.M. thesis, Union Theological Seminary in Virginia, 1970.

_____. "Science, Nature, and Society: A New Approach to James Henley Thornwell." *Journal of Presbyterian History* 50 (Fall 1972): 306–25.

Brandon, Betty Jane. *Alexander Jeffrey McKelway: Statesman of the New Order.* Ph.D. diss., University of North Carolina at Chapel Hill, 1969.

Burhans, David. *A Study and Evaluation of John Leland's Contribution to American Religious Liberty.* M.A. thesis, Southern Baptist Theological Seminary, Louisville, KY, 1966.

Clarke, Thomas Erskine. *Thomas Smith: Moderate of the Old South.* Th.D. thesis, Union Theological Seminary, 1970.

_____. *Wrestlin' Jacob: A Portrait of Religion in the Old South.* Atlanta: John Knox, 1979.

Deschamps, Margaret Burr. *The Presbyterian Church in the South Atlantic States, 1801–1861.* Atlanta: N.p., 1952.

Dewitt, John. "Princeton College Administrations in the Eighteenth Century." *Presbyterian and Reformed Review* 8 (1897): 387–417.

Farmer, James Oscar. *The Metaphysical Confederacy: James Henley Thornwell and the Synthesis of Southern Values.* Macon: Mercer University Press, 1986.

Fraser, A.M. *Dr. Thornwell as an Ecclesiologist, Centennial Addresses Delivered Before the Synod of South Carolina in the First Presbyterian Church, Columbia, October 23–24, 1912 Commemorating the Birth of the Rev. James Henley Thornwell.* Spartanburg, SC: Band and White, 1913.

Garber, Paul Leslie. "A Centennial Appraisal of James Henley Thornwell." *A Miscellany of American Christianity.* Edited by Stuart C. Henry. Durham: Duke University Press, 1963.

_____. *The Religious Thought of James Henley Thornwell.* Ph.D. diss., Duke University, 1939.

Garth, David Kinney. *The Influence of Scottish Common Sense Philosophy on the Theology of James Henley Thornwell and Robert Lewis Dabney.* Ph.D. diss., Union Theological Seminary, 1979.

Hartness, Robert Worley. *The Educational Work of Robert Jefferson Breckinridge.* Ph.D. diss., Yale University, 1936.

Hickey, Doralyn J. *Benjamin Morgan Palmer: Churchman of the Old South.* Ph.D. diss., Duke University, 1962.

Hill, William. *Autobiographical Sketches of Dr. William Hill, Together with His Account of the Revival of Religion in Prince Edward County and Biographical Sketches of the Life and Character of the Reverend Dr. Moses Hoge of Virginia.* Historical Transcript, no. 4. Richmond, VA: Union Theological Seminary in Virginia, 1968.

Hoge, John Blair. *The Life of Moses Hoge.* Historical Transcript, no. 2. Richmond, VA: Union Theological Seminary in Virginia, 1964.

Hollifield, E. Brooks. *The Gentlemen Theologians: American Theology in Southern Culture, 1795–1860.* Durham: Duke University Press, 1978.

Hood, Fred J. *Reformed America: The Middle and Southern States, 1783–1837.* University, AL: University of Alabama Press, 1980.

Hudson, William Emmit. *"The Least of These": The Beneficences of the Synod of Virginia.* Edited by William E. Hudson. Richmond, VA: Presbyterian Committee of Publication, 1926.

Hurley, James F., and Eagan, Julia Goode. *The Prophet of Zion-Parnassus: Samuel Eusebius McCorkle.* Richmond, VA: Presbyterian Committee of Publication, 1934.

Johnson, Thomas Cary. "The Alleged Differences Between the Northern and Southern Presbyterian Churches." Southern Presbyterian, 1894.

_____. *A History of the Southern Presbyterian Church.* New York: Christian Literature, 1894.

_____. *The Life and Letters of Benjamin Morgan Palmer.* Richmond, VA: Presbyterian Committee of Publication, 1906.

_____. *The Life and Letters of Robert Lewis Dabney.* Richmond, VA: Presbyterian Committee of Publication, 1903.

Kay, Martha W. *The Literary Contributions of the Faculty of Union Theological Seminary, 1807–1941.* M.R.E. thesis, General Assembly's Training School for Lay Workers, 1942.

La Motte, Louis C. *Colored Light, the Story of the Influence of Columbia Theological Seminary, 1828–1936.* Richmond, VA: Presbyterian Committee of Publication, 1937.

Lacy, Benjamin Rice, Jr. *Revivals in the Midst of the Years.* Richmond, VA: John Knox, 1943. Reprint. Hopewell, VA: Royal, 1968.

Law, Thomas H. *Dr. Thornwell as a Teacher and a Preacher, Centennial Addresses Delivered Before the Synod of South Carolina in the First Presbyterian Church, Columbia, October 23–24, 1912, Commemorating the Birth of the Rev. James Henley Thornwell.* Spartanburg, SC: Band and White, 1913.

Lewis, Frank Bell. *Robert Lewis Dabney: Southern Presbyterian Apologist.* Ph.D. diss., Duke University, 1946.

Lingle, Walter L. *Presbyterians, Their History and Beliefs.* Richmond, VA: John Knox, 1945.

Liston, R. T. L. *The Neglected Educational Heritage of Southern Presbyterians: The Smyth Lectures.* Bristol, TN: Liston, n.d.

McAllister, J. Gray. "James Smith, A Memorial by the Faculty of Union Theological Seminary." *Union Seminary Record* LII (January 1941): 103–7.

Macartney, Clarence Edward Noble. "James Waddell: The Blind Preacher of Virginia." *Princeton Theological Review* 19 (October 1921): 621–29.

McElroy, Isaac Stuart. *The Louisville Presbyterian Theological Seminary*. Charlotte, NC: Presbyterian Standard Publishing, 1929.

McIlwaine, Richard. *Hampden-Sidney College: Its Relation and Services to the Presbyterian Church, and to the Cause of Education and Religion; a Discourse, Preached at the Second Presbyterian Church, (M.D. Hoge, D.D., Pastor,) Richmond, Virginia, February 5, 1888*. Richmond, VA: Whittet and Shepperson, 1888.

Macleod, James Lewis. *The Presbyterian Tradition in the South*. Oakwood, GA: Educational Enterprises, 1977.

Maddex, Jack P. "From Theocracy to Spirituality: The Southern Presbyterian Reversal on Church and State." *Journal of Presbyterian History* 54 (1976): 438–57.

Matthews, Donald. *Religion in the Old South*. Chicago: University of Chicago Press, 1974.

Maxwell, William. *A Memoir of the Rev. John H. Rice, D.D.* Philadelphia: Whetham; Richmond, VA: Smith, 1835.

_____. "Memoir of Rev. William Graham." *Virginia Evangelical and Literary Magazine* 4 (1821): 75–79, 150–52, 253–63.

Morrison, Alfred J. *The College of Hampden-Sidney: Calendar of Board Minutes, 1776–1876*. Richmond, VA: Hermitage, 1912.

Mulder, John M. "Joseph Ruggles Wilson: Southern Presbyterian Patriarch." *Journal of Presbyterian History* 52 (1974): 245–71.

Nall, J. H. "Benjamin Morgan Palmer, D.D., LL.D." *Presbyterian Quarterly* 16 (July 1902): 77–92.

Opie, John. "The Melancholy Career of 'Father' David Rice." *Journal of Presbyterian History* 47 (December 1969): 295–319.

Overy, David Henry. *Robert Lewis Dabney: Apostle of the Old South*. Ph.D. diss., University of Wisconsin, 1967.

Parker, Harold M. *Studies in Southern Presbyterian History*. Gunnison, CO: B and B Printers, 1979.

_____. *The United Synod of the South: The Southern New School Presbyterian Church*. Westport, CT: Greenwood, 1988.

Pilcher, George William. "Samuel Davies and the Instruction of Negroes in Virginia." *Virginia Magazine of History and Biography* 74 (July 1966): 293–300.

_____. *Samuel Davies: Apostle of Dissent in Colonial Virginia*. Knoxville, TN: University of Tennessee Press, 1971.

"Presbyterians of the Revolution." *Watchman of the South* 3 (February 20, 1840): 104.

Price, Philip Barbour. *The Life of the Reverend John Holt Rice, D.D.* Richmond, VA: Library of Union Theological Seminary in Virginia, 1963.

Rankin, W. Duncan. *James Henley Thornwell and the Westminster Confession of Faith*. Greenville, SC: A Press, 1986.

Reed, R. C. "A Historical Sketch." *Bulletin Columbia Theological Seminary* (Columbia, SC) 18 (October 1925): 5–15.

Robinson, William Childs. *Columbia Theological Seminary and the Southern Presbyterian Church; a Study in Church History, Presbyterian Policy, Missionary Enterprise, and Religious Thought*. Decatur: Lindsey, 1931.

Rogers, Tommy. "James Henry Thornwell." *Journal of Christian Reconstruction* 7 (1980): 175–205.

Smith, H. Shelton. "The Church and the Social Order in the Old South as Interpreted by James H. Thornwell." *Church History* (June 1938): 115–24.

_____. *Studies in Southern Presbyterian Theology*. Amsterdam: Drukkerij En Uitgeverij Jacob Van Campen, 1862. Reprint. Phillipsburg, NJ: Presbyterian and Reformed, 1987.

_____. *Reformed Evangelism*. Clinton, MS: Multi-Communication Ministries, 1975.

Smylie, James H. *A Cloud of Witnesses: A History of the Presbyterian Church in the United States*. Richmond, VA: CLC Press, 1965.

_____. "Presbyterians and the American Revolution." *Journal of Presbyterian History* 52 (1974): 299–488.

Squires, W. H. T. "John Thomson: Presbyterian Pioneer." *Union Seminary Review* 32 (1920–1921): 149–61.

Thompson, Ernest Trice. *Changing Emphasis in American Preaching*. Philadelphia: Westminster, 1943.

_____. *The Changing South and the Presbyterian Church in the United States*. Richmond, VA: John Knox, 1950.

_____. *Presbyterian Missions in the Southern United States*. Texarkana, AR: Presbyterian Committee of Publication, 1934.

_____. *Presbyterians in the South*. 3 vols. Richmond, VA: John Knox, 1963–1973.

_____. *The Spirituality of the Church: A Distinctive Doctrine of the Presbyterian Church in the United States*. Richmond, VA: John Knox, 1961.

Thompson, Robert Ellis. *A History of the Presbyterian Churches in the United States*. New York: Christian Literature, 1895.

Thomson, C.T. "Robert Lewis Dabnew—The Conservative." *Union Seminary Review* 35 (January 1924): 155–70.

Tyler, James Hoge. *The Family of Hoge: A Genealogy*. Greensboro, NC: Hoge, 1927.

Waddel, John N. *Memorials of Academic Life Being an Historical Sketch of the Waddel Family, Identified Through Three Generations with the History of the Higher Education in the South and Southwest*. Richmond, VA: Presbyterian Committee of Publication, 1891.

Waddel, Joseph A. *Annals of Augusta County, Virginia: From 1726–1871*. 2d ed. Bridgewater, VA: Carrier, 1902.

_____. *The Waddells*. Pamphlet. Richmond, VA: Union Theological Seminary in Virginia, 1901.

Webster, Richard. *A History of the Presbyterian Church in America from Its Origin Until the Year 1760, with Biographical Sketches of Its Early Ministers . . . with a Memoir of the Author, by the Rev. C. Van Rensselaer . . . and an Historical Introduction by the Rev. William Blackwood.* Philadelphia: Wilson, 1857.

Wells, John Miller. *Southern Presbyterian Worthies.* Richmond, VA: Presbyterian Committee of Publication, 1936.

Whaling, Thornton. *Dr. Thornwell as a Theologian, Memorial Addresses Delivered before the General Assembly of 1886 on the Occasion of the Quarter-Centennial of the Organization of the Southern Assembly in 1861.* Presbyterian Committee of Publication, 1886.

White, Henry Alexander. *Southern Presbyterian Leaders, by Henry Alexander White . . . with Portrait Illustrations.* New York: Neale, 1911.

Whitlock, Luder G., Jr. "Elders and Ecclesiology in the Thought of James Henley Thornwell." *Westminster Theological Journal* 37 (1974): 44–56.

3. Histories of the Presbyterian Church in the Southern States

Batchelor, Alexander Ramsay. *Jacob's Ladder: Negro Work of the Presbyterian Church in the United States.* Atlanta: Presbyterian Church in the United States, 1953.

Beard, Delamo L. *Origin and Early History of Presbyterianism in Virginia.* Ph.D. diss., University of Edinburgh, Scotland, 1932.

Brown, Katharine Lowe. *The Role of Presbyterian Dissent in Colonial and Revolutionary Virginia, 1740–1785.* Ph.D. diss., The Johns Hopkins University, 1969.

Bullock, James R. *Heritage and Hope: A Story of Presbyterians in Florida.* Edited by Jerrold Lee Brooks. Orlando: Synod of Florida Presbyterian Church in the United States of America, 1987.

Davidson, Robert. *History of the Presbyterian Church in the State of Kentucky: With a Preliminary Sketch of the Churches in the Valley of Virginia.* New York: Carter; Lexington, KY: Marshall, 1847.

Davis, Robert Pickens. *Maryland Presbyterian History.* Th.D. diss., Union Theological Seminary in Virginia, 1958.

_____. *Virginia Presbyterians in American Life: Hanover Presbytery (1755–1980).* Edited by Patricia Aldridge. Richmond, VA: Hanover Presbytery, 1982.

Ellis, Dorsey Daniel. *Look unto the Rock: A History of the Presbyterian Church, U.S., in West Virginia, 1719–1974.* Parsons, WV: McClain, 1982.

Foote, William Henry. *Sketches of North Carolina, Historical and Biographical.* 3d ed. Synod of North Carolina, Presbyterian Church in the United States, 1965.

_____. *Sketches of Virginia Historical and Biographical.* Philadelphia: Martien, 1850.

Garth, John Goodall. *Sixty Years of Home Missions in the Presbyterian Synod of North Carolina.* Charlotte? 1948?

"History of the Presbytery of Hanover." *Evangelical and Literary Magazine* 11 (1828): 531–38, 657–58.

Hoge, Moses D. *Memorial Discourse on the Planting of Presbyterianism in Kentucky One Hundred Years Ago.* Louisville, KY: Courier-Journal, n.d.

Johnson, Thomas Cary. *Virginia Presbyterianism and Religious Liberty in Colonial and*

Revolutionary Times. Richmond, VA: Presbyterian Committee of Publication, 1907.

The King's Business in the Synod of Alabama. Birmingham, AL: Birmingham Publishing, n.d.

Kirk, Cooper. *A History of the Southern Presbyterian Church in Florida 1821–1891*. Ph.D. diss., Florida State University, 1966.

Lodge, Martin Ellsworth. *The Great Awakening in the Middle Colonies*. Ph.D. diss., Berkeley, 1964.

Lowrey, Priscilla M. *The Introduction of Presbyterianism into Mississippi: From the Entrance of Early Presbyterian Settlers to the Formation of the Synod of Mississippi in 1835*. M.A. thesis, Trinity Evangelical Divinity School, 1974.

McGeachy, Neill Roderick. *Confronted by Challenge: A History of the Presbytery of Concord, 1795–1973, Including the Former Presbytery of King's Mountain and Presbytery of Winston-Salem*. Delmar, 1955.

McIlwaine, Richard. *Hampden-Sidney College: Its Relation and Services to the Presbyterian Church, and to the Cause of Education and Religion; a Discourse, Preached at the Second Presbyterian Church, (M.D. Hoge, D.D., Pastor,) Richmond, Virginia, February 5, 1888*. Richmond, VA: Whittet and Shepperson, 1888.

McIlwain, William E. *The Early Planting of Presbyterianism in West Florida*. Pensacola, FL: McIlwain, 1926.

Mahler, Henry Richard, Jr. *The Contribution of Liberty Hall and Washington College to Presbyterianism in Virginia, 1749–1870*. Th.D. diss., Union Theological Seminary in Virginia, 1952.

Marshall, James Williams. *Presbyterian Churches in Alabama 1811–1936: Part I, Sketches of Churches, Outposts, and Preaching Points in the Synod of Alabama Abbeville, Butler, and Megargel*. Edited by Kenneth J. Foreman, Jr. Foreword by William H. C. Frend. Montreat, NC: Cooling Spring, 1985.

Parker, Harold M. *Bibliography of Published Articles on American Presbyterianism, 1901–1980*. Westport, CT: Greenwood, 1985.

_____. *Studies in Southern Presbyterian History*. Gunnison, CO: B and B Printers, 1979.

_____. *The Synod of Kentucky: From Old School Assembly to the Southern Church*. 1975?

Presbyterian Church in the U.S. Executive Committee of Foreign Missions. *Foundations of World Order: The Foreign Service of the Presbyterian Church, U.S.* Richmond, VA: John Knox, 1941.

Presbyterian Church in the US, Synod of Georgia. Executive Committee of Education. *The Task of the Presbyterian Church in Georgia*. Edited by the Synod's Executive Committee of Education. Executive Committee of Education, 1926?

Rice, David. *An Outline of the History of the Church in the State of Kentucky, During a Period of Forty Years: Containing the Memoirs of Rev. David Rice, and Sketches of the Origin and Present State of Particular Churches, and of the Lives and Labours of a Number of Men Who Were Eminent and Useful in Their Day*. Arranged by Robert H. Bishop. Lexington, KY: Skillman, 1824.

Rumple, Jethro. *The History of Presbyterianism in North Carolina*. Historical Transcript, no. 3. Richmond, VA: Union Theological Seminary in Virginia, 1966.

Stacy, James. *A History of the Presbyterian Church in Georgia*. Completed and edited by C. I. Stacy. Atlanta: Westminster, 1912.

Tenney, Levi. *History of the Presbytery of Central Texas*. Austin: Von Boeckmann, 1895.

Terman, William Jennings, Jr. *The American Revolution and the Baptist and Presbyterian Clergy of Virginia: A Study of Dissenter Opinion and Action*. Ph.D. diss., Michigan State University, 1974.

Wilson, Howard McKnight. "The Story of Synod Presbyterians." *Yesterday and Tomorrow in the Synod of Virginia*. Edited by Henry M. Brimm and William M.E. Rachal. Richmond, VA: Synod of Virginia, Presbyterian Church in the United States, 1962.

Wright, Louis B. "Pious Reading in Colonial Virginia." *Journal of Southern History* 6 (1940): 383–92.

4. Southern Presbyterians and Slavery

Alvis, Joel Lawrence, Jr. *"The Bounds of Their Habitations": The Southern Presbyterian Church, Racial Ideology and the Civil Rights Movement, 1946–1972*. Ph.D. diss., Auburn University, 1985.

Bailey, Kenneth K. "Protestantism and Afro-Americans in the Old South: Another Look." *Journal of Southern History* 41 (November 1975): 451–72.

_____. *Southern White Protestantism in the Twentieth Century*. New York: Evanston, 1964.

Berlin, Ira. *Slaves Without Masters: The Free Negro in the Antebellum South*. New York, 1976.

Blassingame, John. *The Slave Community: Plantation Life in the Antebellum South*. New York, 1979.

Christie, John W., and Dumont, Dwight L., eds. *George Bourne and The Book and Slavery Irreconcilable*. Philadelphia, 1969.

Daniel, W. Harrison. "Southern Protestantism and the Negro, 1860–1865." In *Time on the Cross: The Economics of American Negro Slavery*. Edited by Robert W. Fogel and Stanley L. Engerman. Boston and Toronto, 1974.

Eaton, Clement. *The Growth of Southern Civilization, 1790–1860*. New York, 1961.

Green, John C. "The American Debate on the Negro's Place in Nature, 1780–1815." *Journal of the History of Ideas* 15 (June 1954): 384–96.

Jenkins, William Sumner. *Pro-Slavery Thought in the Old South*. Chapel Hill, NC: University of North Carolina Press, 1935.

Jordan, Winthrop D. *White Over Black: American Attitudes Toward the Negro, 1550–1812*. Baltimore, 1969.

Kull, Irving Stoddard. "Presbyterian Attitudes Toward Slavery." *Church History* 7 (1938): 101–24.

MacLeod, Duncan J. *Slavery, Race and the American Revolution*. London: Cambridge University Press, 1974.

Martin, Asa Earl. *The Anti-Slavery Movement in Kentucky Prior to 1850*. Louisville: Standard, 1918.

Murray, Andrew E. *Presbyterians and the Negro—A History*. Philadelphia, 1966.

Norton, L. Wesley. *The Religious Press and the Compromise of 1850: A Study of the Relationship of the Methodist, Baptist, and Presbyterian Press to the Slavery Controversy*. Ph.D. diss., University of Illinois, 1959.

Sherer, Lester B. *Slavery and the Churches in Early America 1619–1819*. Grand Rapids, 1975.

Smith, H. Shelton. *In His Image, But . . . : Racism in Southern Religion, 1780–1910*. Durham, 1972.

Stampp, Kenneth. *The Peculiar Institution: Slavery in the Ante-Bellum South*. New York: Knopf, 1956.

Thompson, Ernest Trice. "Black Presbyterians, Education and Evangelism After the Civil War." *Journal of Presbyterian History* 51 (Summer 1973): 174–98.

Thompson, J. Earl. "Slavery and Presbyterianism in the Revolutionary Era." In *The American Presbyterian Reformed Historical Sites Registry*, no. 41.

Wade, Richard C. *Slavery in the Cities: The South 1820–1860*. New York: Oxford University Press, 1968.

5. General Histories of the Presbyterian Church

Baird, Samuel J. *Assembly's Digest, A Collection of the Acts, Deliverances, and Testimonies of the Supreme Judicatory of the Presbyterian Church from Its Origin in America to the Present Time*. Philadelphia, 1855.

Cheeseman, Lewis. *Differences Between Old and New School Presbyterians*. Rochester: Darrow, 1848.

Crocker, Zebulon. *The Catastrophe of the Presbyterian Church in 1837*. New Haven: Noyes, 1837.

Gillette, E. H. *History of the Presbyterian Church in the United States*. Rev. ed. Vol 1. Philadelphia: Presbyterian Board of Publication, 1873.

Hays, George P. *Presbyterians: A Popular Narrative of Their Origin, Progress, Doctrines, and Achievements*. New York: Hill, 1892.

Hodge, Charles. *The Constitutional History of the Presbyterian Church in the United States of America*. Philadelphia: Martien, 1839.

McGill, Alexander T., Hopkins, Samuel M., and Wilson, Samuel J. *A Short History of American Presbyterianism*. Philadelphia: Presbyterian Board of Publication and Sabbath-School Work, 1903.

Smith, Egbert Watson. *The Creed of Presbyterians*. New York: Baker and Taylor, 1901.

Smith, Elwyn Allen. *The Presbyterian Ministry in American Culture: A Study in Changing Concepts, 1700–1900*. Philadelphia: Presbyterian Historical Society, 1962.

Smith, H. Shelton, Handy, Robert T., and Loetscher, Lefferts A. *American Christianity: An Historical Interpretation with Representative Documents*. Vol. 1. New York: Charles Scribner's Sons, 1960.

Sweet, William Warren. *Religion on the American Frontier*, Vol. II, *The Presbyterians 1783–1840, A Collection of Source Materials*. New York: Holt, 1936.

Thompson, Robert Ellis. *A History of the Presbyterian Churches in the United States.* Vol. 6 of *The American Church History Series.* New York: Christian Literature, 1895.

Trinterud, Leonard J. *The Forming of an American Tradition: A Re-examination of Colonial Presbyterianism.* Philadelphia: Westminster, 1949.

Vander Veld, L. G. *The Presbyterian Churches and the Federal Union.* Cambridge: Harvard University Press, 1932.

Webster, Richard. *A History of the Presbyterian Church in America, from Its Origin until the Year 1760, with Biographical Sketches of Its Early Ministers.* Philadelphia: Wilson, 1857.

Wood, James. *Old and New Theology: or, The Doctrinal Differences Which Have Agitated and Divided the Presbyterian Church.* Philadelphia: Presbyterian Board of Publication, 1855.

Zenos, Andrew C. *Presbyterianism in America: Past, Present and Perspective.* New York: Thomas Nelson and Sons, 1937.

6. Reference Resources

Albaugh, Gaylord P. "American Presbyterian Periodicals and Newspapers, 1752–1830." *Journal of Presbyterian History* 31: 3, 4; 42: 1, 2.

Blackburn, John C. *A Southern Presbyterian Bibliography.* Manuscript. Reformed Theological Seminary Archives.

Beecher, Willis J., comp. *Index of Presbyterian Ministers Containing the Names of All the Ministers of the Presbyterian Church in the United States of America, 1706–1881.* Philadelphia: Presbyterian Board of Publication, 1883.

Bowden, Henry Warner. *Dictionary of American Religious Biography.* Westport, CT: Greenwood, 1977.

Hill, Samuel S. *Encyclopedia of Religion in the South.* Macon: Mercer University Press, 1984.

Lippy, Charles H. *Bibliography of Religion in the South.* Macon: Mercer University Press, 1985.

Morrison, Alfred J. *College of Hampden-Sidney: Dictionary of Biography, 1776–1825.* Hampden-Sidney College, 1920.

Nevin, Alfred, ed. *Encyclopedia of the Presbyterian Church in the United States of America.* Philadelphia: Presbyterian Encyclopedia Publishing, 1884.

Parker, Harold M., Jr. *Bibliography of Published Articles on American Presbyterianism, 1901–1980.*Westport, CT: Greenwood, n.d.

Prince, Harold B., ed. *A Presbyterian Bibliography.* ATLA Bibliography, no. 8. Metuchen, NJ: Scarecrow, 1983.

Scott, E.C. *Ministerial Directory of the Presbyterian Church, U.S. 1861–1941.* Austin: Von Boeckmann-Jones, 1942.

Shulman, Albert M. *The Religious Heritage of America.* New York: Barnes and Company, 1981.

Spence, Thomas Hugh. *The Historical Foundation and Its Treasures.* Montreat, NC: Historical Foundation Publications, 1960.

Sprague, William B. *Annals of the American Pulpit.* Vols. 3 and 4, *The Presbyterians 1783–1840, A Collection of Source Materials.* New York: Holt, 1936.

INDEX

Adger, John, 53, 59, 72, 73, 74
Alexander, A. A., 18, 19, 20, 27, 33, 47
Alexander, Joseph Addison, 57
Alexander, J. E., 23
Aquinas, Tomas, 47
Aristotle, 63
Arminianism, 3, 21, 40, 43, 44
Atonement, 50
Authority, 25, 69

Bahnsen, Gregory, 30
Bancroft, George, 63
Baker, Daniel, 17
Balch, Hezekiah, 23
Barth, Karl, 37
Bavinck, Herman, 19, 33, 37
Baxter, George Addison, 18, 19, 20, 45
Beecher, Henry Ward, 63
Berkeley, William, 16
Blair, John, 17, 18
Boston, Thomas, 59
Boyle, Gaston, 20, 33
Bozeman, Theodore Dwight, 73, 74
Bracket, William O., 72
Breckinridge, Robert, 24
Butler, Joseph, 47

Calvin, John, 45, 50, 59
Campbell, Alexander, 21
Clebsch, William, 56
Come, Donald R., 73
Cunningham, William, 50

Dabney, R. L., 19, 20, 27, 29, 37–60
Davies, Samuel, 17, 18
Dick, John, 45, 50, 51, 52, 59
Dooyeweerd, Herman, 10

Edwards, Jonathan, 45, 52

Finney, Charles, 5, 43
Foote, William Henry, 18, 33
Foreman, Kenneth J., 73
Fowler, Robert Booth, 12

Garber, Paul L., 71
Girardeau, John L., 27, 72, 73, 74
Gomarus, Francis, 50
Goulding, Thomas, 17
Graham, Billy, 2
Graham, Samuel, 39
Graham, William, 18, 19
Griffin, Clifford S., 72

Hamilton, William, 47, 48, 69
Hays, George P., 33
Henry, Carl F. H., 9, 10, 12
Henry, Robert, 69
Hesselink, John, 11
Hodge, A. A., 37
Hodge, Charles, 19, 20, 24, 26, 27, 45, 46, 47, 50–54, 57, 58, 59, 65, 73
Hoge, Moses, 18
Holifield, E. Brooks, 73, 74
Hollis, Daniel W., 72

Humanistic, 44
Hume, David, 47, 48
Hutcheson, Richard, 72

Jackson, Thomas J., 42
Johnson, Terry, 60
Johnson, Thomas Carey, 33, 38, 55, 56, 57, 60
Justification, 18, 21

Kant, Immanuel, 47, 48
Knox, John, 72
Kuyper, Abraham, 31, 38, 47

Lacy, Drury, 19
Lewis, Frank Bell, 43, 44, 50, 56, 57
Liberalism, 27, 54
Loetscher, Lefferts, 73

Machen, J. Gresham, 20, 27, 30
Maddex, Jack P., 74
Makemie, Francis, 16
Marsden, George M., 11, 72, 73
McGready, James, 20
Metcalf, Robert, 31
Meyer, D. H., 73
Moody, D. L., 43
Murray, John, 30, 49, 50, 51

New School Presbyterianism, 18, 22, 23, 26, 40, 64, 65
Niebuhr, H. Richard, 10
Niebuhr, Reinhold, 10

Old School Presbyterianism, 18, 22, 23, 24, 25, 26, 32, 40, 63, 64, 65, 67, 68, 70, 71
Overy, David H., 57, 59, 60
Owen, John, 50

Palmer, B. M., 26, 54, 71
Peck, Thomas, 72

Reid, Thomas, 47, 73
Rice, John Holt, 18, 19, 33
Robinson, John, 18
Robinson, Stuart, 25
Rushdoony, Rousas John, 10, 31, 54

Sampson, Francis, 40
Schaeffer, Francis, 10, 47, 48
Schaff, Phillip, 33
Scott, Otto, 56
Scottish Common Sense Realism, 46, 47, 53, 68, 69, 70, 74
Shedd, W. G. T., 37, 54
Sin, 57, 58
Smith, Adam, 74
Smith, H. Sheldon, 72, 73
Smith, James Porter, 20
Smith, John Blair, 19
Smith, Josiah, 17
Smith, Morton H., 33, 58, 73
Smylie, James H., 56, 57
Smythe, Thomas, 25
Snyder, Howard A., 72
Spencer, Stephen R., 48
Stone, Barton, 21
Stone, William, 16
Stout, Harry S., 12
Stuart, Dugald, 69, 73

Taylor, A. E., 51
Thompson, Ernest Trice, 16, 32, 56, 59, 74
Thornwell, James Henley, 24, 25, 27, 29, 31, 33, 45, 46, 51, 52, 54, 59, 63–74
Torrance, Thomas E., 47, 48, 49, 57
Turretin, Francis, 19, 27, 45, 49, 53, 57

Vander Stelt, John C., 74
Van Til, Cornelius, 29, 46, 47, 48, 51
Vos, Geerhardus, 49, 50

Wallace, Ronald S., 59
Warfield, B. B., 15, 16, 27, 37, 49, 50, 56
Webb, R. A., 27
Whitefield, George, 17, 18
Wilson, Charles R., 55, 60
Wilson, Samuel B., 39
Winter, Ralph D., 72
Witherspoon, John, 68
Wolterstorff, Nicholas, 11